USING
MANORIAL
RECORDS

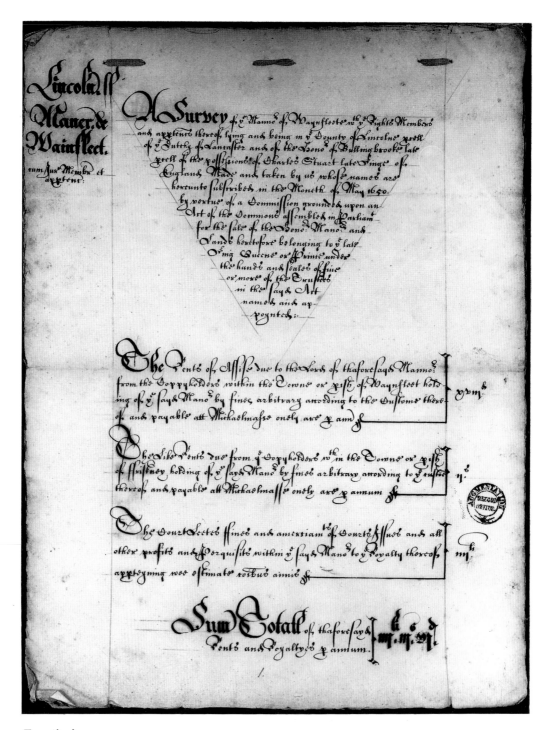

Frontispiece

This illustration is taken from a Commonwealth Survey of the manor of Wainfleet, Lincolnshire, made in 1650. (E 317/Lincs/39).

PUBLIC RECORD OFFICE READERS' GUIDE NO. 6

USING
MANORIAL RECORDS

by
Mary Ellis

PRO Publications
in association with
The Royal Commission on Historical Manuscripts

The Royal Commission on Historical Manuscripts
Quality House
Quality Court
Chancery Lane
London
WC2A 1HP

The Public Record Office
Kew
Richmond
Surrey
TW9 4DU

ISBN 1 873 162 38 3

LIST OF CONTENTS

LIST OF ILLUSTRATIONS

ACKNOWLEDGEMENTS

I am very grateful to Dr Elizabeth Hallam-Smith of the Public Record Office for suggesting this project and to Christopher Kitching and Dick Sargent for allowing me the necessary time away from my duties at the Historical Manuscripts Commission.

A survey of the classes in the PRO which contain manorial records was undertaken by Helen Watt during the summer of 1993 and this was invaluable in compiling the tables in Part Two. Jim Murray of the PRO was of enormous help throughout. The text was read by Alfred Knightbridge and Marion Edwards, and prepared for publication by Melvyn Stainton and Millie Skinns. I am very grateful for their help.

Using the Public Record Office

The Public Record Office (PRO) is at Kew where original records are held.

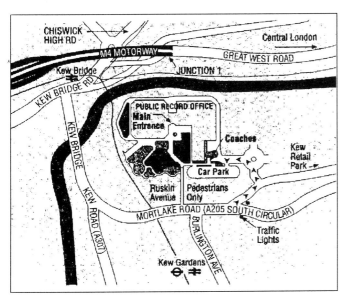

Public Record Office, Ruskin Avenue, Kew, Surrey TW9 4DU.
The telephone number is:
0181-876-3444.

Hours of opening
From 7 April 1997

Monday	9.30am to 5.00pm
Tuesday	10.00 am to 7.00pm
Wednesday	9.30am to 5.00pm
Thursday	9.00am to 7.00pm
Friday	9.30am to 5.00pm

and from 5 July 1997

Saturday	9.00am to 5.00pm

Certain popular classes are viewed on microfilm, and some can be seen at the Office's central London microfilm reading room which is at:

Family Records Centre Myddelton Street, London EC1 1UW.
The telephone number is:
0181-392-5300.

Hours of opening
From 10 March 1997

Monday	9.00am to 5.00pm
Tuesday	10.00am to 7.00pm
Wednesday	9.00am to 5.00pm
Thursday	9.00am to 7.00pm
Friday	9.00am to 5.00pm
Saturday	9.30am to 5.00pm

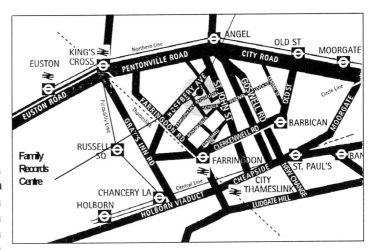

The office at Kew is closed on public holidays and for annual stocktaking (usually the first two weeks in October), but the central London reading room will not close for stocktaking.

When you first visit the PRO, please bring with you formal documentary proof of identity bearing your name and signature. If you are not a British citizen you will need to bring your passport or national identity card. You will then be issued with a Reader's Ticket. Without a valid ticket you cannot be admitted to the reading rooms or order documents. You do not need one to visit the central London microfilm reading room.

You may use only graphite pencils in the reading rooms. Pens of any kind are not allowed. You may use personal computers, typewriters and tape recorders in designated areas. A full list of Reading Room rules is available on request.

Each document has a unique three-part reference. The first part is the lettercode, for example PROB for the records of the Prerogative Court of Canterbury or IR for Inland Revenue, according to the provenance of the documents, but with the growth of bureaucracy the letters given do not necessarily bear any resemblance to the body concerned, eg Council on Tribunals is BL. The second part is the class number, which represents the series within the lettercode. The third part is the piece number, which represents the individual document.

To identify the lettercode and class, consult the published Current Guide, which is the primary guide to the holdings of the PRO. The Current Guide is in three parts. Part 1 describes the history and functions of government departments. Part 2 briefly describes each class with information such as the covering dates and number of pieces. Part 3 is the index to the other two parts. There is no general detailed index covering records in the PRO. Once possible classes have been identified, the next step is to consult the class lists which briefly describe each piece. These are available in the PRO reading or reference rooms.

Records held on microfilm by the central London reading room are as follows:

PROB 6	Prerogative Court of Canterbury Administrations 1796-1857	
PROB 11	Prerogative Court of Canterbury registered copy wills 1384-1858	
IR 26	Death Duty records 1796-1857	
IR 27	Death Duty indexes 1858-1903	
RG 4	Non parochial Registers, registers of births, marriages and deaths 1567-1858	
HO 107	1841-1851 Census returns	
RG 9-RG 12	1861-1891 Census returns	

Errata:

PROB 6 Prerogative Court of Canterbury Administrations 1559-1857

IR 27 Death Duty indexes 1796-1903

PART ONE:

Introducing Manorial Records

INTRODUCTION

From the time of the Norman conquest until well into the seventeenth and eighteenth centuries, the manorial system provided a framework for the lives of much of the rural population of England and a significant portion of Wales. For the local and family historian this is of great importance because the manorial system generated a host of valuable records which can tell us the names of those who lived on particular manors and may also tell us much about their everyday lives. Even after the decline in importance of the system from the seventeenth century many manor courts continued to function as the sole means by which copyhold land was transferred, and records which contain a good deal of genealogical information were, therefore, still being produced right up until the 1920s.

Manorial records are defined in the Manorial Documents Rules as:

> 'court rolls, surveys, maps, terriers, documents and books of every description relating to the boundaries, wastes, customs or courts of a manor'.

In fact any documents produced as a result of the internal administration of a manor fall within the definition of the Rules and all are of potential value to historians. Specifically excluded from the definition in the Rules, however, are documents connected with the title of the manor. Deeds, grants, conveyances and legal records dealing with the ownership of title to the lordship of the manor are not therefore considered as part of this study.

Family historians are, it seems, always being reminded that historical records were not drawn up for their benefit. No historical records were produced for the convenience of historians, but if used with a degree of care manorial records can yield a great deal of useful information for the amateur researcher. At the same time it is important not to have unrealistic expectations. One vital point to recognise at an early stage is that the manorial system did not encompass all of the land in England and Wales. In England some land was never included in a manor and some tenants were never subject to manorial jurisdiction; while in Wales the manorial system itself had only a limited impact. A recognisable manorial system certainly existed in Pembrokeshire, Glamorgan and Monmouthshire, and in those border counties into which Anglo-Norman influences also extended, but for the North Wales counties of Caernarvonshire, Anglesey, and Merioneth researchers will find only traces of the existence of manorial organisation and a corresponding paucity of manorial records.

A further point to consider is that the language of the records may present problems. Medieval manorial records are invariably in Latin which may be heavily abbreviated and although the use of English became more common during the sixteenth century it was by no means universal. If you wish to use manorial records you must therefore be prepared to encounter Latin and to gain some basic skills in palaeography. This may seem somewhat off-putting but it should not necessarily be so. Manorial records were drawn up using established conventions and the general format of particular types of records can therefore be learnt relatively quickly. Sound advice which has been offered by previous writers on manorial records is to start by looking at seventeenth and eighteenth century examples. These will be in English but they deal with similar subject matter to the earlier records and are often laid out in the same fashion. Meanwhile, you can practise your Latin on published versions of older records.

After 1733, Parliament decreed that all administrative records should be written in English so anything after this date should be manageable. By following the advice given above you should soon become familiar with manorial records and this will make it easier to locate the information that you seek. An essential tool for Latin beginners is Eileen Gooder's *Latin for Local History* (Longmans, 2nd edn., 1978). Also, Denis Stuart's recently-published *Manorial Records, an introduction to their transcription and translation* (Phillimore, Chichister, 1992) provides a specialist introduction to reading manorial records. Stuart's book provides excellent exercises in both translation and palaeography and also contains a select dictionary and suggestions for further reading.

It is not the purpose of this book to duplicate the work of Stuart and others. Rather, it aims to make manorial records more accessible to researchers by, firstly, discussing their historical context so that researchers can be more aware of the possibilities of the records in terms of the information which they contain and, secondly, by providing detailed advice on locating the documents themselves. Part One, therefore, provides an introduction to the manorial system and to the records which were produced. Chapter One looks at the nature of the manor, discusses the origins of the manorial system and introduces the various types of manorial tenure. The succeeding chapters look in turn at particular types of manorial records, discuss how and why they were produced and indicate the range of information that they may contain. Part Two is divided into two sections. The first section describes how to locate manorial records using the Manorial Documents Register maintained by the Royal Commission on Historical Manuscripts (HMC). The second section specifically deals with the large quantity of manorial documents in the Public Record Office (PRO) by providing detailed advice on how to use the finding aids available to the public.

CHAPTER ONE:

The Manor and its Origins

What is a Manor?

It is very difficult to provide an adequate definition of an institution which began to emerge before the Norman conquest and which continued to function until the twentieth century. No single definition could be true for all periods or for all manors at a given time. Of the many definitions which have been attempted, perhaps the neatest is that given by the seventeenth-century writer and professional surveyor, John Norden. In *The Surveyors Dialogue,* which he published in 1607, he defined the manor as a:

> 'little common wealth, whereof the Tenants are the members, the
> Land the bulke, and the Lord the head'

This idea of the manor as a community or body of several parts without each of which a manor cannot exist very cleverly encapsulates the essential nature of the manor. But it does not quite equate to the simple idea which is often taught in schools of the manor as a geographical unit.

The traditional picture of a manor is one of a compact area, at the centre of which is the manor house: the lord's residence. Clustered around the manor house would be the village comprising the humble dwellings of the tenants and of course the village church. This centre of population would be surrounded by the fields under cultivation and beyond this would lie any common or waste land which belonged to the manor. The fields for cultivation would be divided into strips shared out between the tenants and the lord. The land held by the lord himself is known as **demesne** land.

Whereas some manors did follow this 'ideal' pattern, others did not. In upland areas of the country 'the manor' may not have been a compact village but rather a group of scattered farmsteads interspersed with land belonging to other manors or with waste land. It should also be remembered that a lord may have owned several manors, only one of which would have been his normal place of residence, and many manors therefore never needed a manor house or **capital messuage** as a lord's manor house and grounds are usually referred to in manorial records. Hence the concept of a manor as a compact geographical unit is in many ways less helpful, and less meaningful, than Norden's view of a manor as a system of social and economic organisation based on tenants holding land from a superior lord.

In order to understand this idea more fully it is useful to look briefly at the historical background of the manorial system and then to look in more detail at the types and conditions of tenure to which manorial tenants were subject. By doing this now we will be able to turn later to the manorial documents themselves and gain from them a much clearer picture of life on the manor than would be otherwise possible.

The Manorial System

The system of relationships between lords and tenants based on the tenure of land probably began to take shape in the period immediately prior to the Norman conquest. In the absence of a strong central government peasants may have seen the advantages of allying themselves to a powerful and influential lord. In return for the protection afforded by this alliance, the lord would have expected some kind of recompense or payment. In some cases the individual seeking protection may have had to surrender his land to the lord and in order to receive his holding back for his own use had to agree to the payment of certain rents or the performance of services, and thereby became a tenant. It is not clear just how far this process had advanced by the time of the Norman conquest but it was certainly not universal. There were still substantial numbers of men who had an acknowledged overlord but who had not surrendered their land to him and could not therefore be considered his tenants.

The Norman conquest, however, brought about a significant change in the relationship between lords and peasants. In the aftermath of his conquest William I had to reward his followers for their military efforts. He accomplished this by granting to them large tracts of land and the Saxon nobility was more or less entirely replaced by a Norman equivalent. For all these momentous changes, the conquest may actually have made very little difference to the everyday lives of those at the lower end of the social scale: their Saxon lord merely being replaced by a Norman one. However, the compilers of the Domesday book now worked on the assumption that all land was held by a lord (known as a tenant in chief) by grant from the crown and that, at a lower level, all land was held by tenants of a lord. Therefore every peasant must be a tenant of one sort or another. Hence they formalised and set down in writing in Domesday the concept of the manor as a discrete unit comprising a lord, his land and the tenants who worked it.

In the remainder of this chapter we will look at two particular aspects of the manor: manorial tenants and, more briefly, the role of manorial administrators. However, before proceeding there is a phrase which we need to explain: that is, **'the custom of the manor'**. This phrase is used by manorial tenants and administrators to describe the set of rules which developed in each of these communities, or manors, to govern the behaviour of the tenants in relation to one another and also in relation to their lord. The provisions of the custom of the manor varied from manor to manor but these 'rules' were essential to the efficient functioning of the manorial system and the phrase necessarily crops up throughout the book.

Manorial Tenure

All manorial tenants were not of equal status. The basic division on the medieval manor was between the free and the unfree tenants. 'Freeholders' held their land from the lord for the payment of a cash rent and, perhaps, also owed light labour services. But apart from the discharge of these obligations they had considerable independence.

The 'unfree' tenants, who were variously referred to as **villeins** or **bondmen** or by some local name, were in a very different position. They too held land from the lord and paid their rents but they were subject to various other obligations. The extent of these obligations depended on the custom of the particular manor concerned; however, they were normally obliged to render labour services or week-work to assist in the cultivation of the lord's demesne land and may have been required to perform other duties such as the repair of the manorial mills or the carting of commodities for sale to market. They may also have had to pay renders in kind, such as butter, eggs, capons or cereals. They were also often subject to severe restrictions on their personal freedom. They could not usually live away from the manor without first obtaining the lord's permission and they often had to make payments for such privileges as allowing their daughter to marry (usually known as **merchet**) or for permission to educate their sons.

Finally, the poorest and humblest on the manor were those who held no land but were employed by the lord or by the more substantial freeholders as labourers. They may have held a cottage with a small garden and were often called **cottars** or **bordars**.

This remained the general pattern of tenure until the fourteenth century and the outbreak of the plague, or Black Death, which devastated the population, and had far-reaching consequences for manorial lords and tenants. With a dramatic slump in the population there was less demand for land and lords had great difficulty in finding tenants to take on holdings. There is no doubt that some land fell out of cultivation and that, for what remained, the tenant's bargaining position was considerably enhanced. Tenants of villein status were able to bargain for the land and also to demand greater security in the form of deeds which set out the terms and conditions of their tenure. At the same time, the restrictions on their personal freedom became more difficult to enforce and eventually declined out of existence.

Over time, villein tenants came to be known as customary holders because they were said to hold their land according to the custom of the manor. By the sixteenth century there were therefore two main types of manorial tenure - freehold and customary hold - but both free and customary tenants could also hold land by a third type of tenure: that is, by lease. Not every manor would include examples of all three categories. For example, on some manors there would have been no freehold land while on others all land would be free and none customary. It should also be noted that tenants could hold land by a combination of these tenures: customary holders could take on additional land by lease; freeholders seem to have been quite happy to take on customary land if the terms were sufficiently favourable. There was certainly no stigma attached to the holding of customary or 'unfree' land by the sixteenth century.

In manorial documents, therefore, you will come across references to tenants and the type of tenure by which they held their land. Knowing the meaning of these references will help you to understand the conditions prevailing on the particular manor in which you are interested and will tell you something about the status of particular individuals and the extent of their participation in the life of the manor. Hence it is worth considering tenure in a little more detail before turning to the documents themselves.

Freeholders

Freehold land was usually held by a tenant for a rent, the level of which had been agreed and fixed in the medieval period and which the lord of the manor had no subsequent right to review. In addition to the payment of a rent, freehold tenants were normally obliged to attend the manor courts, where they may have been required to serve as jurors, to pay a **heriot** on the death of a tenant (usually the best living or 'quick' beast on a holding or, if there were no beast, a money payment: usually 5 shillings). They normally also owed **relief**, which was a cash payment made to the lord of the manor by the heir to, or purchaser of, freehold land and it was often set at the value of one year's rent. Other than the discharge of these obligations, the freehold tenants were largely independent of the manorial system. Unlike the customary tenants they were not subject to restrictions on their personal freedom imposed by the custom of the manor and they had the right to sell or dispose of their land as they wished without reference to the manorial courts.

By the sixteenth century inflation had taken a toll on the value of rents paid by freeholders and, in many cases, their rents no longer formed a significant proportion of the income of a manorial lord. They were therefore of less interest to the manorial officials who were responsible for administering and securing the lord's dues than customary tenants and consequently less attention was paid to them when manorial records were compiled. Nevertheless if you are looking for a family believed to be manorial freeholders they may make fleeting appearances in any of the records that you find.

Customary Tenants

These were by far the most numerous tenants in England and Wales. By the sixteenth century a large proportion of customary land was known as **copyhold** land and the terms are here used interchangeably. The term 'copyhold' refers to the practice of giving a tenant a copy of the court roll entry which detailed his admission to his holding, and which served as proof of his title. This procedure developed out of the fact that any change in ownership of customary land had to be conducted through the manor courts and recorded on the manor court rolls. However, because the customary tenant was subject to the custom of the manor the specific terms and conditions under which he was allowed to hold the land differed from manor to manor and could even vary between groups of customary tenants on a single manor. The possible variants in customary tenure were therefore enormous but they can, for convenience, be sub-divided into two basic types: customary holders of inheritance and customary holders for life or lives.

Land held by customary holders of inheritance descended to an heir whose identity would be determined by the custom of the manor: whether it be by primogeniture to the eldest son, to the youngest son or to several people who shared in some form of partible inheritance or gavelkind. (The latter was prevalent in Kent and also in Wales.) On the other hand, as the name suggests, customary tenants for life or lives had an interest in their land during their life only, or for a limited number of lives, (usually three), including, perhaps, the tenant, his wife and one of their children. When the life or lives expired the land reverted to the lord who could then grant it out to a tenant of his choice.

By the sixteenth century customary tenants did not normally owe extensive labour services because these had largely been commuted to cash payments. Like the freeholders they would owe a heriot and suit to the manor courts. In addition, however, customary tenants also owed a payment known as an **entry fine**. This was due upon an incoming customary tenant and, according to the custom of the manor, may have been either fixed or arbitrary. Where the custom of the manor decreed that the level of the entry fine was arbitrary, the lord could demand whatever sum the market would bear. This was obviously to the disadvantage of smaller and poorer tenants who had less opportunity to accumulate capital to pay a large entry fine and, gradually, during the sixteenth and seventeenth centuries it became more accepted that entry fines should be 'reasonable'. The level was often set at the sum of one or two years' rent.

In certain circumstances a customary tenant might be liable to forfeit his holding to his lord. Customary tenants were usually required to maintain their holdings in good condition and this often applied to hedges and ditches as well as to the dwelling house and farm buildings. Failure to do so, in theory, could mean the loss of the holding.

Finally, there were some restrictions on the rights of customary tenants. The right to exploit minerals on customary holdings was normally reserved to the lord of the manor and the tenants were normally forbidden to cut down timber, other than for the essential maintenance and repair of buildings.

Leasehold

Leasehold was first used on manors for the letting of demesne land. This was simply because the terms which could be demanded for land let out in this way were not restricted or fixed by the custom of the manor. Former demesne land could therefore be let out by lease for rents which represented the true market value of the land and which could be regularly reviewed. Because of this, manorial administrators were often very careful to set down details of leasehold land separately in their records.

Leasehold could also be used to let out **extent land**, which was the term used for land which had been newly brought into cultivation, and other assets besides land, such as mills and the right to exploit natural resources by means of quarries, lime pits, iron ore or coalmines. In the medieval period leases tended to be granted on an annual basis but by the sixteenth or seventeenth centuries they were more often granted for a period of twenty one years or three lives which, rightly or wrongly, was considered to be an equivalent length of time. It was reckoned that this was a sufficient period to give the lessee the security necessary to encourage him to invest in and improve the land, while the lord could still review the rent at regular intervals.

The terms by which land was leased out were set by the lord of the manor. A fine was normally imposed for granting or renewing a lease and an annual rent would be payable. In addition the lord could also require from the tenant payments in kind such as capons or hens and could impose obligations such as the grinding of corn at the manorial mill. On the death of a tenant a heriot might also be payable. Rights to the exploitation of minerals and timber were usually reserved to the lord of the manor.

Because of the opportunities offered by leases for regular reviews of rents and the freedom of the lord to set the terms and conditions, leasehold became an increasingly popular form of tenure and significant numbers of customary tenants were persuaded to take up leases. The process by which this was achieved is not clear from manorial records but the possibility that a degree of coercion was used cannot be discounted. On the other hand customary holders for life may have welcomed the security offered by a lease.

Tenants at Will

A final class of tenants which you may encounter in manorial records are the tenants at will. These tenants were among the poorest and the most vulnerable inhabitants of a manor. They usually held a cottage with a small close or garden attached which they had probably erected without leave on the manorial waste land. Upon discovery by manorial officials, these tenants would normally be allowed to continue to occupy their cottages but a rent would be imposed and their tenure would be entirely dependent upon the goodwill of the lord.

Sub-Tenants

As we have already said, manorial tenants commonly had the right to sub-let their land. This has some important implications for the use by researchers of rent rolls and rentals. While the compilers of manorial surveys and other records were very particular about recording the names and details of the manorial tenants, they frequently saw no reason to record the names of the sub-tenants who actually occupied and worked the land. It is, therefore, entirely possible that an individual worked far more land than is apparent from a rent roll simply because, as well as land held directly from the lord of the manor, he may have held additional land by sub-letting. By the same token, if you believe that an individual was resident in a manor but can find no reference to him in the extant rent rolls it may be that he was a sub-tenant and no record of his holding has been made. There is the further possibility that a particular tenant held land in several manors and the rent roll of one manor may well not reveal the true extent of the land held by that individual.

It should be evident from the above that the administration of a manor was a complex business. The various types of tenure and the rules governing land holding meant that manorial lords had to establish a suitable mechanism which ensured that their rents were collected and that all services due were rendered. In simple terms, this led to the emergence of manorial officials with various responsibilities and to the eventual production of written administrative records.

Manorial Administration

In one of the earliest hand books on estate management called *The Seneschaucy* (which was probably composed about 1276) the anonymous author lists the officials who ought to serve on a manor and the duties they ought to perform. It provides a useful insight into the surprisingly sophisticated functioning of a medieval manor.

The chief officer was the **steward** who may have acted in this capacity for a group of his lord's manors. According to *The Seneschaucy* the **bailiff**, appointed by the lord, acted as the 'general manager' and looked after the day to day running of the manor. A **reeve** would also be appointed to act as a 'foreman' with particular responsibility for overseeing the cultivation of the land held by the lord in the manor. The reeve would normally be a tenant who would receive no remuneration but would be excused the payment of his rent and services during the period of his appointment, which would usually be for one year. Other officials included the **hayward** - who supervised the making of hay and harvesting - and various minor officials such as the **pinder** who was the keeper of the manorial pound (or pinfold). There would of course have been variations to suit the needs of individual manors but certainly the steward and the bailiff were common to most manors by the thirteenth century and it was a part of the responsibility of these officials to produce and keep surveys and account rolls as one of the means to ensure efficient administration.

Apart from their administrative duties these officials would also have had a role to play in the regulation of life on the manor. It was inevitable that as the manor developed as a social and economic unit disputes between tenants arose and that anti-social behaviour had to be deterred, where possible, and punished whenever it occurred. So far as we can establish, meetings of the manor were therefore convened at intervals to address these problems and in the course of time these developed into the formal sessions of the manor courts. The first indication of the operation of such meetings are found in manorial account rolls where the fines imposed as punishments for misdemeanours against the common good are noted as part of the income of the lord. By the late thirteenth century written records of these meetings survive in a form which we can recognise as court rolls.

In terms of their origins therefore manorial records can roughly be divided into two types: records associated with the administration of the manor as a source of revenue for the lord, and court records. The first group consists mainly of surveys - that is custumals, extents and rentals which detail the income that the lord was entitled to receive - and the accounts which detail the financial state of the manor and the income that he actually received. The second group consist of the court records which detail the process of regulating the manorial community. The following chapters examine each type of record in some detail and consider their potential uses and limitations for researchers.

CHAPTER TWO:

Early Surveys and Accounts

Introduction

The primary purpose of a manorial survey was to provide for the lord of the manor a written record of the obligations owed to him by his tenants. Surveys are the oldest form of manorial records and the fact that isolated examples survive from the Saxon period indicates that the principle of maintaining a written record of dues was appreciated at a very early stage in the development of the manorial system. The payments of cash rents, of commodities or renders in kind, and of labour services owed to a manorial lord constituted a significant proportion of the income he received from his manor and the effort of making a written checklist of them, in a period when very few written documents of any kind were produced, was clearly felt to be worthwhile.

However, while manorial surveys were principally drawn up at the instigation of the lord as an administrative tool, they also provided for the tenants of the manor a record of the extent of their liabilities. This means, in effect, that the rights of the tenants, as well as those of the lord, were defined because the lord could not demand more from his tenants by way of labour services or rent than that which was specified in the survey. Surveys also recorded - and thereby protected - the rights which the tenants of a manor were entitled to enjoy, such as access to common land for grazing. Hence the survey defined and protected the position of the tenants equally as much as it did that of the lord.

It is evident from the above that surveys contain a great deal of information which will be of use to local and family historians. For the family historian interested in a particular manor the survey will usually contain a list of all the tenants who held land in that manor. It will also detail the land held, the type of tenure under which it was held and the rents, renders and services which the tenant paid. If you are fortunate, the survey will also amplify this information and will tell you something of the restrictions imposed by the custom of the manor under which your ancestor lived. This information is equally useful to the local historian but, in addition, surveys also contain many details about field and place names, the existence of mills, mine works and so on. Surveys compiled from the mid-sixteenth century may also contain descriptions of the boundaries of the manor which are a further source of valuable topographical information.

In this and the following chapter we are going to look in more detail at the use and interpretation of the information contained in surveys. In order to do this effectively it is useful to look at surveys in chronological order because we can then see how the type and level of the information which they contained changed as the purposes for which they were drawn up shifted over time. The next chapter deals with the highly detailed surveys of the sixteenth century and later, but here we will look at the surveys of the medieval period and begin by defining the basic types of surveys to be found.

Custumals

In its earliest and most basic form the survey was an inventory detailing all the various types of revenue which the lord was entitled to receive from his tenants. This type of survey is usually known as a custumal and it simply set out the names of all the tenants, along with the details of the land which they held and particulars of the rents, labour services and payments in kind which each of them owed to the lord. A brief recital of the customs of the manor may also be included. They were made in the twelfth and thirteenth centuries and most surviving examples are for manors which formed part of large ecclesiastical estates. Many examples of custumals have been published.

Extents

Whereas custumals were solely concerned with the obligations of tenants, the earliest extents - which represent the first development of the survey - began to include some details relating to the demesne land of the manor. Demesne is the term applied to the land which was held by the lord himself and not let out to tenants. The land would be worked on the lord's behalf by a combination of hired labour and tenants rendering labour services.

The inclusion of a description of the demesne land in surveys is significant because it marked a crucial change in the economic situation in the thirteenth century. Inflation, and in particular rising food prices, meant that there were increasing profits to be made from agriculture and if lords were to maximise their profits then they needed accurate information about the land which they were working. The surveys which resulted from this development are known as extents.

The practice of compiling manorial extents seems to have originated with the royal practice of compiling an **inquisition post mortem** on the death of a tenant-in-chief. A tenant-in-chief was someone who held land directly from the crown. An inquisition post mortem would be drawn up by royal officers and would briefly detail and value the land so that an appropriate payment could be levied, for the royal coffers, on the heir to the property before he was allowed to take possession of his inheritance. Inquisitions post mortem are not manorial records but they had an effect on the form and content of manorial surveys in that the set format of the inquisition post mortem was taken and utilised by manorial officials when drawing up their own records.

All the items on the manor were described and valued in a set order, beginning with the manor house and demesne land and concluding with the tenants' rents and services. Extents are therefore often described as 'valued surveys' but it is vital to be aware that the total valuation given for the manor is not its capital value - that is, it is not the amount of money the lord would gain if he sold the manor - but the total that could be gained if the manor were leased out for one year. This may seem odd but historians have explained extents by suggesting that the lords who commissioned them needed the information so that they could make decisions about how best to manage their estates. By establishing the annual value of a manor, a lord could decide whether it was more profitable to work the demesne land or to let it out for rent.

By the fourteenth century the economic situation had changed. There was less incentive (less profit) for manorial lords to work their demesne land and, on the whole, the lands were leased out for rents, either in a number of blocks or parcels or as a single unit to lessees in return for the payment of a cash rent. Naturally, once the decision to lease rather than work the land had been taken there was little reason for the compilation of extents detailing the demesne holdings on behalf of the lord. Surveys from the later fourteenth century and fifteenth century therefore tend to be briefer documents detailing the rents that the lord was entitled to collect. This type of survey is usually known as a **rental**. *Figure 1* (LR 13/18/26) is a good illustration of a rental. It relates to the manor of Gillingham, Dorset, for the year 1618. It is an unusual document in that after the tenants and their rents have been listed the manorial officials have also included a list of residents of the manor and it therefore offers a rare opportunity to identify persons who are living but are not tenants on a manor.

Another aspect of these changing economic circumstances was that if the lord was not cultivating his demesne land then he did not require the services of his tenants.

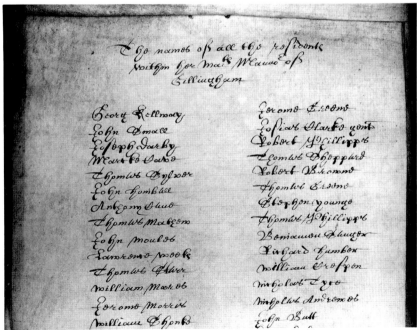

Figure 1 - An extract from a rent roll (or rental) of the manor of Gillingham, Dorset, made in 1618 which includes a list of the residents of the manor. (LR 13/18/26)

After the decline in demesne agriculture, therefore, labour services were often exchanged for a money payment, or **commuted**. Taken together with the rent this money payment was referred to in manorial documents as a **quit-rent**.

It should not be imagined that all surveys made conform to this rather neat chronological progression. Examples of extents, for example, may be found later than the fourteenth century, but this gives a general overview of the surveys that the researcher should expect to find dating from the period before the sixteenth century.

Accounts

As we have seen, the increased use of extents coincided with the period of demesne agriculture because of the value landowners placed upon working, rather than letting, their land at that time. For similar reasons the period of demesne agriculture also saw the development of manorial accounts. The lord would expect his bailiff and his reeve not only to collect his rents but to keep a financial account of the farming of the demesne land and to keep a careful check on money paid out and money received for the sale of commodities at market.

Manorial accounts are based on what is known as a 'charge and discharge' system. Manorial account rolls begin with the 'charge' which, in simple terms, was the money the manorial officials should have gathered from rents, from profits made by the sale of commodities, from the imposition of fines made in the manor courts, and from the payment of heriots. The 'discharges', which are listed after the charges, are the out-goings relating to, for example, the purchase of seed corn for sowing or equipment and the payment of hired labour. The balance, or profit, is the difference between the charge (income) and the discharge (out-goings or expenses) and this is the sum that the manorial lord would expect to receive from his officials. On a large landed estate the money would be collected by an official known as the lord's receiver who would be responsible for the collection of money from several manors and may have kept his own written account of the revenue he collected for rendering to the lord. These are referred to as **receiver's accounts**.

Manorial accounts are among the most difficult manorial records to use and to interpret and there is insufficient room here for the full discussion that they require. The researcher is therefore advised to consult a more detailed study, such as P D A Harvey's *Manorial Records of Cuxham, Oxfordshire, c. 1200-1359* (London, 1976) which contains an extensive introduction and explanation of manorial accounting and also includes transcripts of Cuxham manor accounts. Further examples of accounts will be found in *Accounts and Surveys of the Wiltshire lands of Adam de Stratton*, edited by M W Farr (Devizes, 1959).

The decline in demesne agriculture also saw the general decline of the keeping of manorial accounts. However, it was usual for manorial officials to continue to keep some record of the rents paid by manorial tenants. These documents are known as **rent rolls** or sometimes confusingly as **rentals**, but their purpose is to record the actual amounts paid by the tenants rather than the amounts due from them. It is necessary to examine any document of this nature that you come across in order to determine the type of information that it contains. Rent rolls simply list against the tenants' names the rent that they have paid. Although they are usually very brief, these documents can be useful in that they will give details of all the manorial tenants on a particular manor.

CHAPTER THREE:

Later Surveys

Introduction

For a variety of reasons the sixteenth century saw a major surge in the production and use of manorial surveys. The large amount of land sold in the aftermath of Henry VIII's dissolution of the monasteries allowed the purchase of landed estates by a whole new class of people, many of whom had a commercial background and who were keen to exploit efficiently their newly purchased land. Established landowning families too had to look to the administration of their estates. A period of severe inflation made it essential for land to be managed efficiently if incomes were to keep pace with rising prices and their efforts to improve administrative practices led to a considerable increase in the amount of records produced, while having a particular effect on surveys. They became long and extremely detailed descriptions of all aspects of the manor as landowners sought to record in minute detail the particulars of every potential source of revenue which a manor might yield, and to identify areas where revenue might be increased.

The documents which survive from the sixteenth and seventeenth centuries are of enormous value to local and family historians because of the amount of detail they contain. Before exploring these details, however, it is worth spending a little time looking at how a survey was made because understanding the process of making surveys can be a great help when it comes to appreciating their contents. In the first instance, following the process through explains why the surveys took the form that they did and, secondly, it helps to bring to life these sometimes long and complex documents.

The process of making a survey

As mentioned in the previous chapter, medieval surveys were probably made at meetings of the manor court. By the sixteenth century, however, the making of a survey had assumed greater formality and the surveys were made at extraordinary meetings of the manor known as the **court of survey.** Hence the surveys normally open with the phrase:

> 'A court of survey held [date]for [name of lord] lord of the manor of...'

The court of survey could be either a meeting specially convened for the purpose of compiling a survey, or it might be held as an adjunct to a normal session of the manor court. You may also come across the record of a **court of recognition** which was the first session of the manor court held after the advent of a new lord. It seems to have been usual on some manors, at the new lord's first court, for all the tenants to acknowledge their new lord and then for their obligations to him to be recorded on the court rolls of the manor. The court of recognition seems to have disappeared by the seventeenth century - being displaced by the court of survey - but the advent of a new manorial lord either by inheritance or purchase remained one of the most common occasions for making a survey.

The court of survey would be conducted either by the steward of the manor or by a group of people commissioned by the lord to make a survey on his behalf. These men were usually senior and trusted members of his household and they were referred to as **commissioners of survey.** The lord would issue a document called a **commission to survey** which gave the commissioners the authority to hold a court of survey and compile a survey on his behalf. Commissions to survey are quite rare but, if you do find one, it may be very useful as it will include any specific instructions from the lord to the surveyors and may shed light on any particular reasons for the drawing-up of the survey.

In the light of the lord's instructions, **articles of enquiry** would then be compiled. The articles of enquiry were a list of questions which would be put to the tenants of a manor at the court of survey. The answers to the articles of enquiry would form the survey. They are sometimes to be found attached to the survey itself and where this occurs it is much easier to understand the answers given. Sadly, however, they rarely survive.

The steward and bailiff would be responsible for ensuring that the tenants of the manor assembled at the given time. The court would be presided over by the steward or the leading commissioner and their first task would be to impanel a jury of survey. The number of jurors varied from around twelve to twenty or more and there does not seem to have been a set procedure for selecting them. They would, however, have been tenants of the manor and we can reasonably conclude that they would be respected and articulate members of the local community. Sir John Perrot, for example, said that jurors for the surveys of his manors should be:

> 'divers of them good freeholders and gentlemen and the rest men of
> good substance and discretion and such as are duyleye experienced
> in the sayd customes'.

The list of those serving as jurors is usually found after the opening preamble of the survey.

The jury would be expected to make their answers to the articles of enquiry in open court before the assembled tenants, and individual tenants could also be called upon to make statements on particular points. All of the tenants would then need to show to the surveyors the various copies and leases by which they held their land so that the details could be recorded for the survey in a rent roll. Here the jury might be called upon to supply details if a tenant had not attended the court or if there were some kind of dispute. The answers to the articles of enquiry and the details of the tenants and their rents would probably be noted down as rough notes by a clerk and would later be written up on to a parchment roll or into a volume. At the end of a survey you may find the signatures, or marks, and seals of the individual jurors who have signed the survey as 'a true and perfect record'.

The contents of surveys

Having looked at the basic procedure for making a survey we can now turn to the wealth of detailed information which they contain. Following on to some extent from the process of making a survey, the information can be sorted into three basic types:

- a description of the boundaries of the manor;

- a presentment by the jury of survey relating to the customs of the manor;

- a rent roll or rental of all the tenants of the manor giving their names, details of the land they hold, by what tenure and for what rent.

Although the description of the boundaries is often the first item dealt with in the survey it is appropriate to leave this aside for the moment as it can be considered more effectively as part of a discussion of later developments of the survey which are dealt with in the next chapter. We shall, therefore, look firstly at the answers or presentments made by the jurors to the articles of enquiry relating to the customs and rights of the manor and then at the rent rolls.

The presentment

To see just how much information the answers presented by the jury to the articles of enquiry can provide to the researcher, simply consider that any or all of the following details might be contained in any one presentment:

- the means by which customary land was inherited and the provision made for a widow of a customary tenant: for example, inheritance by the eldest or the youngest son or that a widow should be permitted to retain a specified portion of a holding so long as she did not re-marry;

- the level of entry fines and heriots paid by the customary tenants, as well as the conditions under which land was forfeited to the lord;

- the level of relief paid by freeholders on alienation or inheritance of land;

- the frequency of court meetings and, occasionally, notes on some of the court practices and proceedings;

- the officials which the manor ought to have, how they should be elected, for what period of time they should serve and what payment they should receive;

- the rights retained by the lord for himself: such as fishing or hunting, or even such things as the right to swarms of bees found on the manor;

- the right of the lord to profit from any treasure trove found on the manor and the right of wreck: that is the right to claim the cargo of ships wrecked along the foreshore of the manor;

- the right to exploit any minerals such as iron ore, coal, or stone quarries and, perhaps, details of how these rights were being exploited; if the rights were leased out, the survey might state the name of the lessee and also the level of profit derived from them;

- the existence of any common land, along with the extent of the privileges which the tenants enjoyed on such land: common land was usually quite strictly regulated; each tenant may have been entitled to graze a certain number of animals on the common and sometimes they had to make a payment for this privilege;

- the entitlement of tenants to take timber, lime or similar building materials from the manor;

- the existence of manorial mills, and the tenants who owed suit to the mill.

All of these items were potential sources of revenue for the lord and might therefore be considered by the court of survey. Hence presentments may be extremely long. They were, however, usually written in English and they give a very clear, if rather static, picture of the situation which pertained on a particular manor at a given time. A phrase often used by the jurors in response to the articles of enquiry is that the customs described had existed 'time out of mind according to the custom of the manor', but researchers should not imagine that the customs did not evolve to meet changing circumstances and a series of surveys for the same manor can show the progress of these changes in their presentments.

Rent Rolls

Often the longest part of a survey is the rent roll, or rental as it is sometimes called. This is the list of all the tenants who held land in the manor, together with the details of the land they held and the rents that they paid. The tenants are usually dealt with by type of tenure and in a large manor may be further sub-divided and dealt with on a parish-by-parish basis. It is possible that the tenants may have been dealt with geographically by tenement but there may be no *apparent* logic to the way in which these lists are ordered. It is unlikely, particularly in earlier documents, that they will be alphabetical and it is rarely a simple matter to locate specific individuals.

Tenants of all types owed suit to the court of survey so that details of their land and the terms under which they held it could be accurately recorded. The commissioners would, no doubt, have had access to other records of the manor to compare the information provided by the tenants. The copyholders would have brought their copies of the court roll, leaseholders would have brought their leases, and freeholders would have brought whatever documents relating to their title that they possessed. For the lord, the manorial officials would probably have had lease books, and registers of the surrenders and admissions to copyhold land.

With all this information to hand, and with the jury of survey available in cases of difficulty, a rent roll could be compiled. The level of detail contained in the surveys varies considerably, but in some cases rent rolls include an enormous amount of useful historical information. For example, the terms and conditions of individual leases may be set out item by item, while much can be learned about the quantity of land held by an individual, or the type of land. *Figure 2* (LR 2/206 f 90) is taken from the rent roll of a survey made in 1618 for the Prince of Wales of his manor of Manorbier and Penally, Pembrokeshire. It relates to the 'husbandry tenants' which

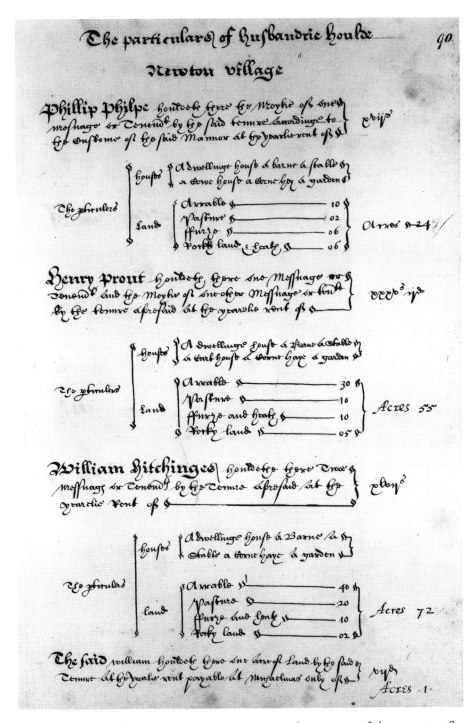

Figure 2 - An extract from a rental made as part of a survey of the manor of Manorbier and Penally, Pembrokeshire, in 1618. (LR 2/206 f 90)

was the local name for the customary tenants of inheritance. As the example shows, for each tenant the surveyors have set down not only the total amount of land held and the rent paid, but also the quantities of the various types of land. Henry Prout, for example, holds a total of 55 acres, 30 acres of which is arable, 10 acres pasture, 10 acres furze and heath, and 5 acres is classed as 'rocky land'. Details of the buildings on each of the holdings are also noted: Henry Prout has a house and garden, a barn, a stable, a cart house and a corn store.

In addition to noting the actual rents paid by a tenant, the rent roll may also note the **improved value**. This reflects the current market value of the land and serves as an indicator of what rent the lord could demand when, for example, renewing a lease. The entry fines imposed on customary tenants were also often set at the value of one or two years' 'improved rent'.

Some rent rolls are much briefer. Indeed, they may only give the names of the tenants and, rather than setting out the terms of a lease, merely refer to the lease books or records of surrenders and admissions for fuller information. This may be very frustrating for the researcher if it transpires that these documents have not survived.

The interpretation of surveys

Although it was the task of the jury to make their answers to the articles of enquiry that favoured neither the lord on the one hand nor the tenants on the other, the temptation to use the survey to improve the lot of themselves and their fellow tenants must at times have been difficult to resist. When looking at a survey you should always bear in mind that manorial tenants were often surreptitiously attempting to improve their lot, particularly on manors where the lord was not resident, and manorial officials were perhaps not as diligent as their lord would have wished. The jury might conceal things from the surveyors and may have attempted to claim rights to which they were not entitled. At best, the jury of survey would be cautious in their answers: at worst, they may have been prepared to lie.

It was this particular problem that prompted John Norden to remark acidly about a jury of survey for Oswestry in Shropshire in 1602 that:

> 'it may be they forget or would not be drawne to remember the acustomed duties and services they owe unto the Lord'.

Commonwealth or Parliamentary Surveys

A final group of surveys which must be mentioned are the Commonwealth or Parliamentary surveys which are preserved in the PRO. Following the defeat of the royalist cause in the Civil War, money was urgently needed by the Parliamentary government to settle the arrears of army pay. In order to raise the necessary revenue an act of Parliament was passed in July 1649 to permit the sale of the manors and other lands previously held by the king and the royal family. Trustees were appointed to oversee the sale and, in turn, the trustees appointed local surveyors to survey the land which was to be sold. A registrar was also appointed to keep a record of sale transactions and to issue deeds to purchasers.

The local surveyors were issued with a model survey and they were instructed to make surveys of the crown lands in their local areas. Two copies of each survey were made, one of which was lodged with the Surveyor General. The other was used by the trustees to assemble the particulars which formed the basis of the sale contracts. The surveys were drawn up for the purposes of valuation and the surveyors were consequently more interested in recording the profits which were generated by, say, the manor courts, the mills, or the rights to hold markets or fairs than with any description of the customs.

However the surveys are still of great value since they list the names of the tenants of the manors with their rents and may provide a variety of incidental information. For the manor of Hogsthorne in Lincolnshire, for example, the surveyors note that no courts have been kept in the manor for many years, and that twenty acres of land have been lost from the manor by the 'irrupcion' of the sea. Finally, an added bonus for contemporary researchers is that because they were compiled during the period of the Commonwealth these surveys are entirely in English.

The copies of the surveys retained by the Surveyor General are preserved in the class **E 317**. An example, from the Commonwealth Survey of the manor of Wainfleet, Lincolnshire made in 1650 is reproduced as the frontispiece to this book. Those used by the trustees will be found in class **LR 2**. There are, however, some duplicates in **DL 32** and occasionally copy surveys will also turn up among private estate collections.

CHAPTER FOUR:

Boundaries, Quantities and Maps

Introduction

So far we have considered the value of surveys to those interested in the inhabitants of a manor in terms of their identities and the conditions under which they lived their everyday lives. For those with an interest in local topography, however, surveys should not be neglected.

Many surveys from the sixteenth century onwards contain detailed descriptions of the boundaries of manors which were often defined by reference to particular physical features of the landscape. They also contain a great deal of information on the quantity of land held by tenants, and the amount of, for example, common or woodland within a manor. The information relating to quantity, however, must be handled with care. Land measurement was, at least up until the late sixteenth century, a primitive science and many manorial lords were, in any case, content to have surveys compiled on the basis of estimated quantities until as late as the eighteenth century.

During the later sixteenth century a small number of manorial lords went to the trouble and expense of employing professional surveyors and cartographers to make maps of their lands. Maps presented information relating to the manor and its tenants in a convenient and immediately accessible format and they eventually came to replace written surveys as administrative tools. It is appropriate therefore to end this chapter with a brief look at manorial maps.

Boundaries

Manorial boundaries were frequently marked by natural features such as rivers or brooks, outcrops of rock or even trees, or by man-made features such as roads or buildings. Moreover, the description of the boundaries may also state the names of the parishes in which the manor lay and the names of adjoining manors and parishes. In rural areas where the landscape is little changed it may therefore be feasible to establish the manorial boundaries, to some extent at least, by using the description given in the surveys. Where possible, by cross-referencing the description to maps, such as the tithe or later estate maps, you may be able to establish an even clearer picture of the boundaries.

Topographical details of this nature are found in later surveys because, as mentioned in the last chapter, it was often a part of the surveyor's task to make a 'perambulation of the bounds' - or as contemporaries called them 'the meares and bounds' - of the manor accompanied by the manorial officials and representatives of the tenants. There seems to have been three reasons for this exercise: to define and record the boundaries of the manor; to ensure that no encroachments of the boundaries were being made by the lords or tenants of adjoining manors; and to check that none of the features which marked the boundaries of the manor had either been moved or removed. The making of a description of the boundaries of a manor was not, however, exclusively confined to the occasions when surveys were compiled and descriptions of manorial boundaries may occasionally be found as individual documents.

Researchers should be aware that the process described above may present a misleading picture. As indicated at the beginning of the book, manors were not always compact units. They could include pieces of land detached from the main body of the manor or could comprise a series of scattered farms. To take an extreme example, the manor of Millwood in Glamorgan was entirely composed of scattered parcels of land which were administered together as a 'manor'. A jury of survey impanelled in 1584 claimed that they were unable to make a statement of the boundaries of the manor because the various tenements were too dispersed. In this case, and in others, researchers may simply have to accept that the boundaries of a particular manor cannot be reconstructed. In more sparsely populated areas of the country, where settlements were interspersed by large areas of rough land and common grazing, then precise manorial boundaries may never have been fixed and, again, cannot be re-constituted.

Quantity and Land Measuring

The modern researcher not only faces difficulties when attempting to define the boundaries of a manor but also when considering the quantity of land held by the lord or by any of his tenants. All surveys contain information about the quantity of land held by tenants and they may also contain information about the amount held as demesne land or about any common, waste and woodland in the manor, but it is no simple matter to interpret this information.

The use of land measuring in the medieval period was very limited, and the equipment and techniques available were undoubtedly crude. Nevertheless there is evidence to suggest that parcels of demesne land which were let out by manorial lords were measured prior to leasing. By the sixteenth century there was a noticeable trend for surveys to be made which included precise information on the quantities of land held by tenants. The major reason for this was the enclosure movement. Manorial tenants were increasingly keen to create consolidated holdings rather than farm a number of scattered strips of land while sharing common pasture land with other tenants. This process of exchanging the scattered strips of land, and of dividing and enclosing common pasture, inevitably led to disputes over the equity of exchanges and the quantities of land allocated. This resulted in the frequent need to employ a land measurer to compile a measured survey.

In the first chapter we also discussed the advantages to the lord of introducing leasehold tenure where possible since it was not subject to the restrictions imposed by the custom of the manor, such as a fixed rent. It was to the lord's advantage to have potential leasehold land measured so that the actual quantity of land to be leased was known and an appropriate rent could be demanded.

However, although there was a large increase in the use made of land measurement, many manorial lords seem to have been content with cruder methods of determining quantity. Information in the rent rolls of surveys frequently relies on estimates made by the jury of survey and the tenants and such estimates could, of course, be misleading. A salutary example comes from a 1609 survey of the manor of Halcetor, Montgomeryshire. When asked, the tenants estimated the area of Corndon forest to be 200 acres. It was almost certainly nearer to 600 acres: a margin of error of 200%!

Even when the quantities given in surveys were the product of measurement, the amounts stated must be handled with care. In the first instance the use of the word 'acre' was not always as straightforward as one might expect. A statute of 1305 established a standard acre of an area 40 perches long and four perches wide, based upon a perch of 16½ feet. However, in reality the size of the perch was subject to a plethora of local variants and there were also variations in the number of perches required to make up an acre. These acres which differed from the standard acre were known as 'customary acres' and could vary enormously in size. Interpretation of quantity can therefore be problematic if a document does not give an indication of the dimensions of the acre in use. In some parts of the country a local customary acre could still be found in use even in the nineteenth century.

Manorial Maps

We have already established that a manorial survey was a written description of a manor, the compilation of which usually required the surveyor to examine the deeds and evidences by which manorial tenants held their land, to ensure that the answers given to the articles of enquiry were truthful, and, perhaps, to walk the bounds of the manor. The social and economic changes of the sixteenth century, however, gradually began to exert pressure for greater precision in the art of surveying and this, in turn, led to changes in the nature of the survey and the function of the surveyor. The introduction of land measurement, as discussed above, was a significant development. The production of written surveys accompanied by maps was the next step and, eventually, written surveys were superseded by maps altogether.

There was a noticeable increase in the production and use of maps generally from the sixteenth century and the publication of, for example, the county maps produced by Christopher Saxton drew the attention of land owners to the usefulness of maps as a means of defining and presenting in an easily digestible format the limits and boundaries of their manors. The universal adoption of maps as tools of manorial administration was, however, a gradual process. The earliest manorial maps seem to have been drawn up when there was a dispute over boundary limits or when, for whatever reason, boundaries had to be defined more precisely than usual. In other words there had to be a particular set of circumstances in which a map would be considered useful. Sixteenth century manorial maps are therefore a rare find for the researcher.

Examples of this type of map were produced when the profession of cartography was still very much in its infancy. Many of the 'maps' produced in this period are, in reality, more akin to pictures: there may be no scale and the documents may not even be the product of a properly measured survey. This, however, reflects the fact that they were intended not so much to depict accurately the topography of an area, as we would expect from a modern map, but to strengthen an argument by illustration. We can take as an example a map of Leathley manor in Yorkshire, drawn up in 1596.

Some kind of dispute appears to have arisen concerning the extent of the jurisdiction of the Leathley manor courts over tenants who lived within the bounds of the forest of Knaresborough. There also seems to have been a further question over the rights of Leathley manor tenants to take turves and to pasture their cattle in the forest. There was, therefore, a need to define the boundary of the forest and, as *figure 3* (MPC 238) shows, this is marked on the map. However, while the map is, on the one hand, merely a crude illustration of the boundary position it also contains a good deal of incidental information which is of great historical value. Several villages are marked on the map by means of thumb-nail sketches of houses and the village church. The drawings of the churches are probably the earliest known representations of the buildings. A mill is also shown and, more unusually, a standing cross is marked.

Although the map is orientated to the north, no scale is used and it is obviously not the work of a skilled cartographer. Nevertheless it is still of great historic interest as well as being an extremely attractive document. Maps of this type cannot give information of the same quality as later documents but they may still be of use to the researcher providing, for example, the earliest representation of a building and valuable architectural information. In other cases these early maps may reveal the existence of mills, weirs, fish stews, ponds, bridges and other interesting topographical features.

Figure 3 - A map of the manor of Leathley, Yorkshire, made in 1596. This map is also reproduced in colour on the front cover. (MPC 238)

Later maps

More sophisticated information may be extracted from manorial maps which were the product of a properly measured survey and were drawn to scale. The use of such maps increased from the seventeenth century, although it is important to be aware that some manors and estates in England and Wales were not mapped until the eighteenth or even the nineteenth century. For those manors where maps were made, however, the maps can provide a wealth of information. Most obviously they define the boundaries of the manor concerned. They will also normally contain information on the type of land in a manor (wood or park land for example), on the utilisation of this land, and on the agricultural organisation of the manor. Maps of the seventeenth and eighteenth centuries are often very useful in revealing, for example, the extent of the process of enclosure.

Apart from these topographical details, later maps also frequently contained the names of the tenants who held land within the manor. Sometimes this information was written into a book of reference which accompanied the map but on other occasions it was incorporated onto the map itself. *Figure 4* (MPA 24) is a map of the manor of Little Leighs Hall made in 1609 by John Walker and his son: the famous Essex map makers. The map delineates fields and notes the field names; woodland is marked and, more interestingly, two small parcels of 'hop ground' are identified; roads, water courses, houses, the church and church yard are also shown. The table at the top right of the map names all the customary tenants who hold land in the manor and indicates the quantity and location of the land that they hold. The table at the bottom left identifies the demesne land of the manor, which totals 296 acres, 2 roods and 31 perches, and serves to illustrate a point made earlier about the care manorial officials took to keep separate account of this type of land.

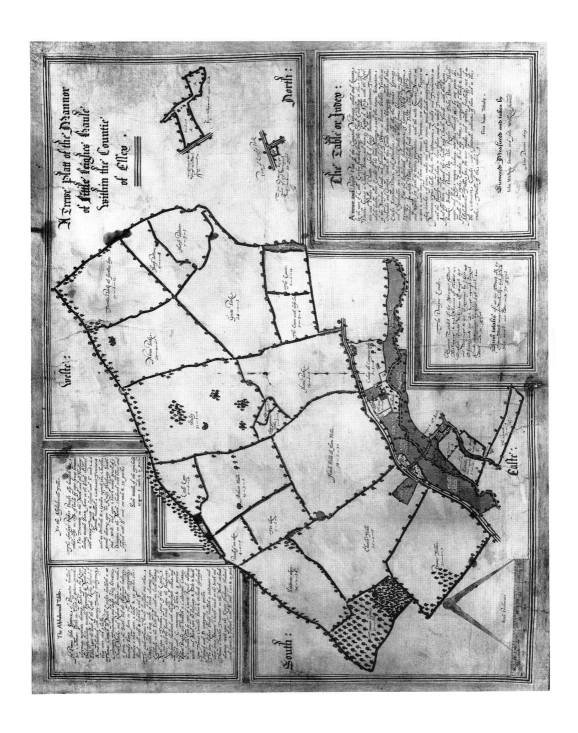

Figure 4 - A map of the manor of Little Leighs Hall, Essex, made in 1609. (MPA 24)

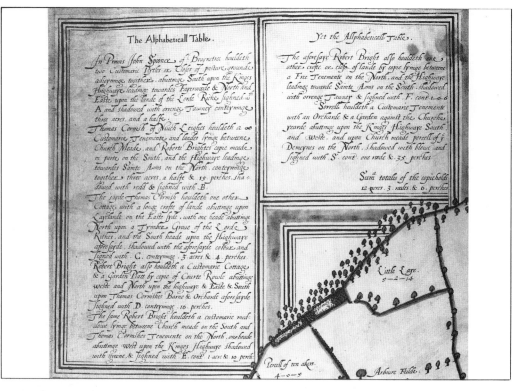

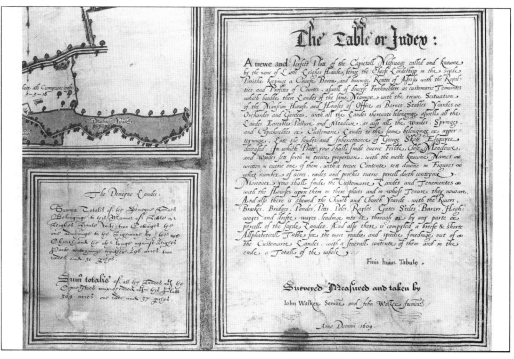

Figure 5 (MR 977) is a mid-seventeenth century map of the manor of Garstang, Lancashire which illustrates effectively the problems of interpreting land measurements in manorial documents. The map shows all the fields in the manor and assigns to each one a reference consisting of a letter and a number. A table at the bottom of the map, reproduced in detail overleaf, gives the field names and also the size of these fields and parcels of land in both statute and customary measurements. T 6 (Wood Field alias Birches), for example, which appears mid-way down the second column, measures 4 acres, 19 perches of statute measure, while it is only 2 acres, 2 roods and 7 perches of customary measure. The total land in the manor according to statute measure is 474 acres, 119 roods but 292 acres, 3 roods, 18 perches customary measure.

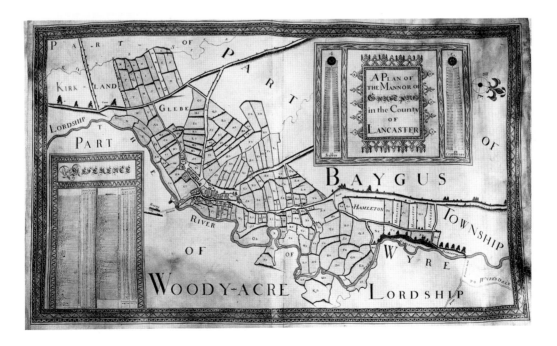

Figure 5 - A map of the manor of Garstang, Lancashire, made in the mid-seventeenth century. (MR 977). The table of field names and measurements is enlarged overleaf.

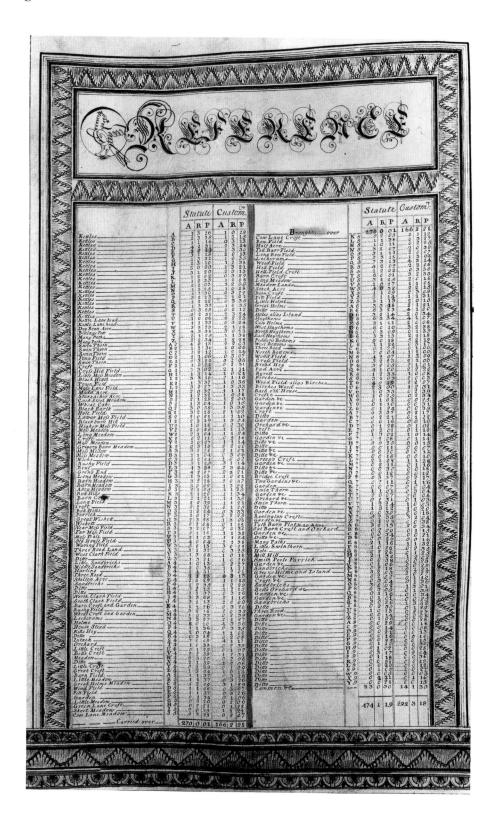

CHAPTER FIVE:

The Manor Court and its Records

Introduction

In 1641 Sir Edward Coke in *The Compleat Copy-Holder* said that the central court of the manor, the court baron,

> 'is incident to, and inseparable from, a Manor...[and] is the chief Prop
> and Pillar of a Manor, for that no sooner faileth, but the Manor falleth
> to the Ground'.

This quotation does two things. Firstly, it re-enforces the idea established in Chapter One that the manor was a social rather than a geographical concept and, secondly, it emphasises the key role that the courts played in the manorial system.

While manorial surveys tell us a great deal about lords and tenants on particular manors and about the relationships between them, the picture they present is a limited one. Surveys set out the provisions of the custom of the manor which were, in effect, the ground rules for life on the manor. But setting down the custom of the manor in a survey was no guarantee that the ground rules would be respected at all times and a judicial system was, therefore, needed to consider possible infringements of manorial customs and to punish offenders. Hence the manor courts came into existence and the records that they generated enhance what can be learnt from the surveys by providing intriguing and informative glimpses of actual events in the day-to-day lives of manorial tenants.

As with many other types of historical record, manorial court documents can be used directly without any awareness of the reasons for their compilation. They can certainly be used to link particular individuals to manors without too much difficulty, but much more can be gained from the records with an understanding of how and why they were produced. For example, many of the records follow an established pattern because of the standardised ways in which they were compiled and a knowledge of this pattern is a useful guide to the whereabouts in the documents of the information that you seek. Similarly, much can be learned about the status, wealth and behaviour of individuals from court records but this depends, at least in part, upon an understanding of where in the documents the names appear and why. In order to achieve this it is necessary, first of all, to establish in some detail what the manorial court system entailed.

There were normally two types of manorial court: the view of frankpledge and court leet, and the court baron. Manorial tenants of all types normally owed suit to both of these courts. The view of frankpledge and right to hold a court leet represented the transfer of jurisdiction usually exercised through the royal courts to the manorial lord, and, as they were royal courts, the records will sometimes state that the court was being held in the name of the king rather than that of the manorial lord. The court baron was the court responsible for the internal regulation of the manor. While the court baron continued to function on a significant number of manors up until 1925, by the seventeenth century the court leet was rapidly losing any meaningful role and soon afterwards disappeared in all but name. Because of its earlier decline therefore it is convenient to consider the court leet first.

The View of Frankpledge and Court Leet

One of the responsibilities most frequently devolved from royal jurisdiction to the manorial lord was the view of frankpledge. This was the twice yearly inspection by the sheriff of the county (the sheriff's tourn) of the system of tithings. Each tithing consisted of ten men who had a mutual responsibility for their good behaviour and were represented at the sheriff's court by a tithing-man. If the view of frankpledge was devolved to the manorial lord, the tithing-man would report to the manor court rather than to the sheriff and the lord had to right to impose fines if, for example, it was found that an individual did not belong to a tithing or if the frankpledge had been broken. The view of frankpledge and court leet were normally held twice a year most commonly around Easter and Michaelmas (25 September).

Much of the significance of the system of tithings was lost before 1500 but the view of frankpledge persisted long after this date. Among the records of the manor and hundred of Cheltenham, Gloucestershire, for example, there exists a list of the officials elected and sworn in at a court held on 30 October 1753. Among the officials sworn in are several tithing men.

The manorial lord might also be granted the right to try offences normally dealt with by the royal courts and these, again, would be dealt with in a court leet. For example, manorial lords might be granted the right to administer the assize of bread and ale. This was the responsibility to ensure that bread and ale were produced to a sufficient standard and that short measures were not sold. The court leet was also frequently responsible for the election of constables who were supposed to oversee law and order and in some cases manorial lords were even granted the right to try and execute felons caught red-handed on their manor. However, by the late fourteenth century the leet had been deprived of the power to try serious offences, although it maintained the right to present offences to be referred to the royal assize courts. The sixteenth-century Tudor reforms in justice, especially the system of JPs and the Quarter Sessions, further undermined the position of the leet court and the amount of business brought to the courts rapidly declined.

Although in theory there was a clear distinction between the jurisdiction exercised through the leet and baron courts, in practice this distinction was not always maintained. Separate series of court rolls were not usually kept for the leet court and the record of sessions of the leet were simply recorded on the rolls kept for the court baron. In the court rolls the court leet or (curia leta) will sometimes be referred to as the curia magna, or great court, while the court baron or curia baronis is sometimes called the curia parva, or small court. During the medieval period the record of the proceeding of the manor courts were normally written on parchment rolls; from the sixteenth century however it became more common for court proceedings to be written in a volume. It is not unusual for a court roll or book to record the proceedings of the courts of several manors owned by the same lord and administered by the same steward. The language of the records varies from manor to manor. Latin is, of course, used for medieval records, however again from the sixteenth century some records were kept in English or even in a mixture of Latin and English. On some manors the use of Latin continues right up to 1733 after which date Parliament decreed that all administrative records should be written in English.

The Court Baron

As Coke's comment suggests, the court baron was integral to the manor. In fact one of the tests which lawyers applied to establish the existence of a manor by 1500 was to determine whether or not it had a court baron. The name 'court baron' apparently derives from the fact that the original granting of manors with the right to hold a court would have been made to the king's barons, hence 'court baron'. The fact that the grant of a court was a royal prerogative is important because it meant that an individual who owned land and let it out to tenants could not simply create his own manor by setting up a court and making his tenants subject to 'manorial' jurisdiction.

Although normally just referred to as the court baron, in theory the lord was entitled to hold a **court baron and court customary**. The court baron was supposed to deal with the freeholders while the court customary was for the customary tenants. However, in practice both were dealt with at a single session of the court. The frequency of meetings was governed by the custom of the manor and intervals of every three weeks or every month are most common, although fortnightly intervals are not unknown. On the other hand, on some manors the court only met when there was business to transact.

It was the role of the court baron to administer the regulations set down as the custom of the manor and to deal with offences against it. It also dealt with debts, trespass and disputes between tenants where the value of the damages was less than 40 shillings. Crucially, as we saw when discussing tenure, the court baron also recorded the surrender and admission to customary land and this was the major factor in its survival into the twentieth century. As the business of the court baron was more or less the same in all manors, the process of holding a manor court and of dealing with these matters tended to conform to a set pattern. Consequently the records produced were remarkably similar. Gaining an understanding of the process of holding a manor court therefore makes the task of locating information in the court rolls considerably easier.

The process of holding a manor court

It is relatively easy to reconstruct the process of holding a manorial court. There is, of course, the evidence to be gathered by looking at the records themselves, but the researcher can also turn to the numerous text books or manuals produced for the benefit of manorial stewards. One of the most heavily-used examples of this type of book is *The Compleat Court Keeper* by Giles Jacob. It was first published in 1713 and it contains a detailed description of the method of holding a manorial court and gives numerous examples of the format of particular types of document which a manorial steward might need to use in the course of his duties. Researchers who have a particular interest in the technicalities of holding a manor court will find Jacob immensely valuable.

The first stage in the holding of the court would be for the steward, who was the official responsible for presiding over the court, to issue an order - or as it is usually known a **precept** - to the bailiff of the manor concerned. The purpose of the precept was to give notice to the tenants that a court was going to be held. It would normally contain various practical details relating to the type of court and the time and place of the session. By the eighteenth century, precepts were quite often pre-printed forms with blank spaces left for the details of time and place to be filled in.

Once the court was assembled, the steward would call the tenants to order and begin the business of the court. After the standard opening, giving the name of the manor, the date, the name of the lord in whose name the court is being held and the name of the steward presiding, the first significant items on the manor court rolls are the details of tenants who have not attended the court and who are paying **essoins**. This was a payment made by a tenant who owed suit to the court instead of attending (it was delivered by a proxy). The level of the essoin was usually fixed by the custom of the manor at a few pence but if this was not so, and it was left to the steward's discretion, it could be more severe. It was also often the case that a tenant could not essoin himself for more than two or three successive courts, and there might thus be a note of whether this was the first or second essoin against the tenant's name.

Tenants who did not attend the court and who did not send their excuses could be subjected to a heavier penalty. After the names of the tenants who have essoined themselves, therefore, there will be the names of any tenants who are in default. Such tenants were liable to a fine, or, as fines imposed by manorial courts are usually known, an **amercement**.

The names of the jurors will be the next thing set out in the court roll. The selection of the jury is an area of court procedure which is by no means clear. It may be that notification of the requirement to serve as jurors was given before the day of the court but it is also possible that they may have been chosen on the day of the court itself. For a leet court the number of jurors was usually twelve but for a baron court the number was much more variable. If a leet and baron court was being held at the same time, separate juries may have been impanelled for the two courts but more often than not one jury served for both.

After the jury had been sworn in by the steward the next business of the court was making the **presentments**. This was done by the jury who were required to state - or 'to present' - the various matters which were to be dealt with by the court. Sometimes the court rolls state not that 'the jury present' but that 'the homage present'. This can be confusing but it is merely an expression used to indicate that the jury are making their presentments on behalf of all the tenants ('the homage') and not just themselves. According to *The Compleat Court Keeper,* there were up to sixty potential offences which the jury might present for the consideration of a court leet. For the court baron there could be anything up to forty.

The procedure for making presentments is, again, not entirely clear but it is possible that the jury were selected a few days before the actual court session and that the presentments were prepared and written out in advance. This may explain why in some court rolls the presentments are given and are followed by the decisions of the court, whereas in others the decisions only are given. In the latter cases it is clear from references to the fines imposed on offenders that presentments were made but, for whatever reason, they have not been copied into the court roll.

Presentments

In later records, after the fourteenth century, the matters dealt with in the presentments were various but usually of a petty nature. They could be minor disputes between tenants which had, perhaps, led to limited outbreaks of violence or incidents where the damage caused was less than the value of 40 shillings. Behaviour against the common good was also dealt with, such as the neglect of a tenant to repair his hedges thus leading to damage caused by straying animals, or the failure to clear ditches. Abuses regarding common land were also a frequent source of annoyance: tenants might be guilty of grazing more animals than custom decreed or of attempting to enclose portions of the common for their exclusive use. A tenant might also take timber from the lord's wood or commit a myriad of other minor abuses of the manorial custom, all of which would be presented and dealt with by the court baron. *Figure 6* (LR 3/40/5 f2) shows the presentments made in the manor of Hampton Court in 1662. The offences range from complaints regarding the erection of a fence and the turning of a water course in the hare warren by the late Oliver Cromwell, to encroachment and enclosure of common and waste land, and to the forfeiture of a lease by a tenant for non-payment of rent.

For all offences against the custom of the manor, if found guilty by the steward (who acted as the judge), the tenant might be amerced. Depending on the manor, the level of amercements might be fixed or left to the discretion of the steward. In order to ensure that the level of the fine was considered fair, **affeerors** chosen from among the tenants would be appointed to sit for the court. They had the power to reduce a fine or amercement if they considered it to be excessive. For example, at a court

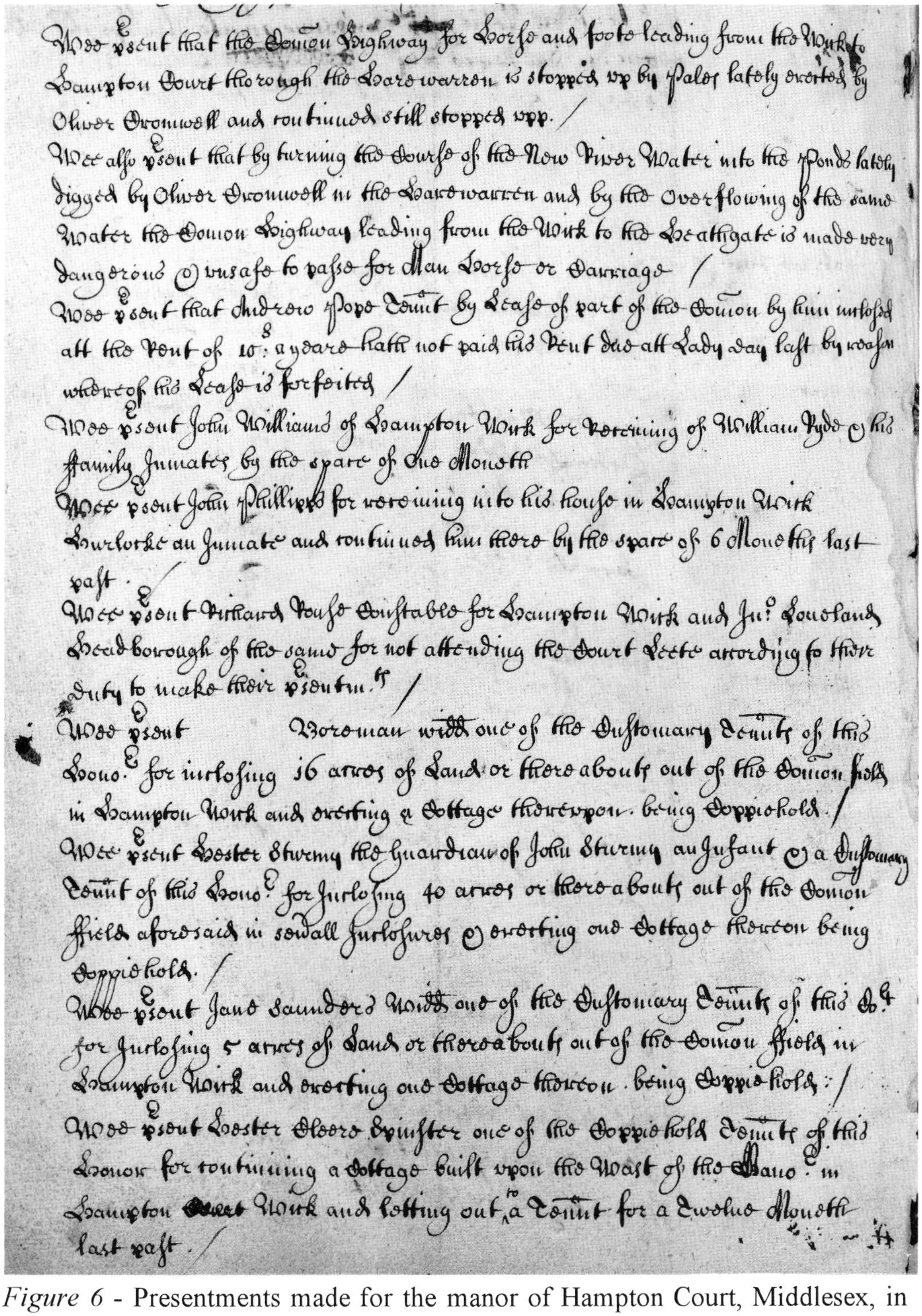

Wee present that the comon highway for horse and foote leading from the Work to
Hampton Court thorough the Hare warren is stopped up by pales lately erected by
Oliver Cromwell and continued still stopped upp. /

Wee also present that by turning the course of the New River Water into the ponds lately
digged by Oliver Cromwell in the Hare warren and by the overflowing of the same
Water the comon highway leading from the Work to the Heathgate is made very
dangerous & unsafe to passe for Man horse or Carriage /

Wee present that Andrew Pope Tennt by Lease of part of the Comon by him inclosed
att the Rent of 10: a yeare hath not paid his Rent due att Lady day last by reason
whereof his Lease is forfeited /

Wee present John Williams of Hampton Work for receiving of William Ryde & his
family Inmates by the space of one Moneth

Wee present John Phillipps for receiving into his house in Hampton Work
.... an Inmate and continued him there by the space of 6 Moneths last
past

Wee present Richard Pouse Constable for Hampton Work and Jn: Lousland
Headborough of the same for not attending the Court Leete according to their
duty to make their presentmts /

Wee present .... Boroman widd one of the Customary Tenents of this
Lrds for inclosing 16 acres of Land or there abouts out of the Comon field
in Hampton Work and erecting a Cottage thereupon being Coppiehold /

Wee present Hester Sturmy the Guardian of John Sturmy an Infant & a Customary
Tenant of this Lrds for inclosing 40 acres or there abouts out of the Comon
field aforesaid in sevall inclosures & erecting one Cottage thereon being
Coppiehold /

Wee present Jane Saunders widd one of the Customary Tenents of this Lrds
for inclosing 5 acres of Land or thereabouts out of the Comon field in
Hampton Work and erecting one Cottage thereon being Coppiehold /

Wee present Hester Gleere Spinster one of the Coppiehold Tenents of this
Lrds for continuing a Cottage built upon the Waste of the Mano.r in
Hampton Work and letting out a Tennt for a twelve Moneth
last past /

Figure 6 - Presentments made for the manor of Hampton Court, Middlesex, in
1662. (LR 3/40/5 f 2)

baron held for the manor of Muchland with Torver, Lancashire on 8 May 1752 Richard Helm was presented at the court for allowing twenty sheep to pasture in a field called Horse Close. For this he was originally amerced 3s 4d but the affeerors reduced the level of the payment to 2s 6d.

The meeting of the manor court also seems to have been used on some manors as an opportunity for the making and re-stating regulations which are known as **ordinances** or **pains**. These provide a good illustration of the importance of the manor court in the regulation of communal agriculture and *Figure 7* (C 116/1) is a good example of the type of issue that they dealt with. They were made at a session of the court baron of the manor of Hartshorne alias Blundells and they deal mainly with the regulation of the common land of the manor, laying down the number of animals the tenants are allowed to loose onto such land, and the times during the year when the animals should be allowed to graze. They also deal with the making of ditches and other issues of common concern to the tenants, such as forbidding any tenant to let loose a 'mangey' or infected horse upon the common. Penalties for breaking the individual ordinances are also set down.

The Manor Courts and Tenure

For customary tenants the manor courts fulfilled a further and important function. Whereas freeholders could dispose of their land without reference to the manorial lord, the customary tenant who held land 'by the will of the lord according to the custom of the manor' was in a very different position. Legal action regarding his land had to be pursued through the manor courts, and manor court rolls and books therefore contain a huge amount of information relating to transactions involving customary land. New tenants could only take possession of customary land through the process of **surrender and admission** which was conducted in the manor court

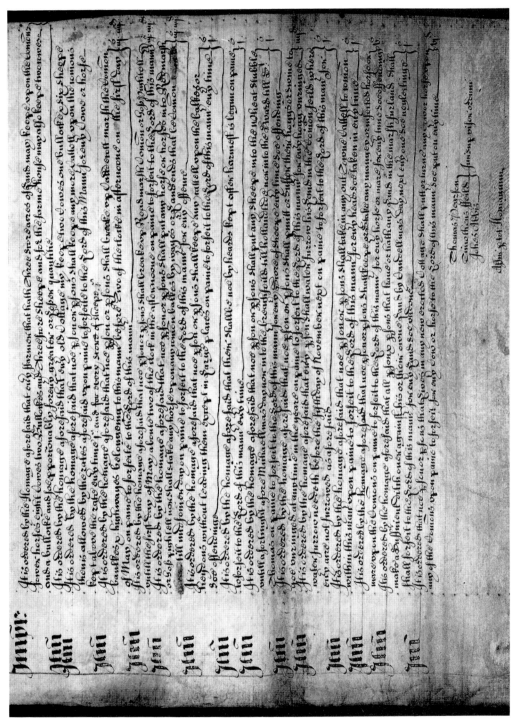

Figure 7 - Pains and Ordinances made in the court baron of the manor of Hartshorne alias Blundells, Bedfordshire, in the seventeenth century. (C 116/1)

and recorded in the manor court rolls.

At a session of the court baron, therefore, the jury were obliged to present the death of any tenants so that a heriot could be collected for the lord and, in the case of a customary or copyhold tenant, so that the heir could come forward to seek admittance to his holding. The death of a tenant might be proclaimed two or three times at successive court meetings but it was customary for a holding on some manors to be forfeit to the lord if the heir did not seek admittance within a specified period, often a year and a day.

The admittance of a new tenant usually took the form of a ceremony conducted between the steward, acting on behalf of the lord, and the tenant (or his attorney) whereby the tenant would grasp a stick or rod held by the steward in open court. This signalled his admittance and the ceremony presumably explains the origins of the description of customary tenants holding by the 'rod' or 'verge'. *Figure 8* is a photograph of a rod which was used for this purpose in manor of Church Aston, Shropshire, in the nineteenth century. An account of the surrender and admission would then be written onto the manor court rolls and a copy also given to the tenant as his own record of his title. The document given to the tenant is referred to as a **copy of court roll**.

The details of these admissions are potentially extremely valuable to the family historian. The record of a surrender and admission will contain the name of the tenant who has died, in some cases with the date and other details of his original admission, and the name of the tenant who is being admitted, along with the details of the relationship, if any, between the out-going and in-coming tenant. The details given in the accounts of the surrender and admission of copyholders for several lives can be particularly valuable since the various ages of the tenants for life will normally

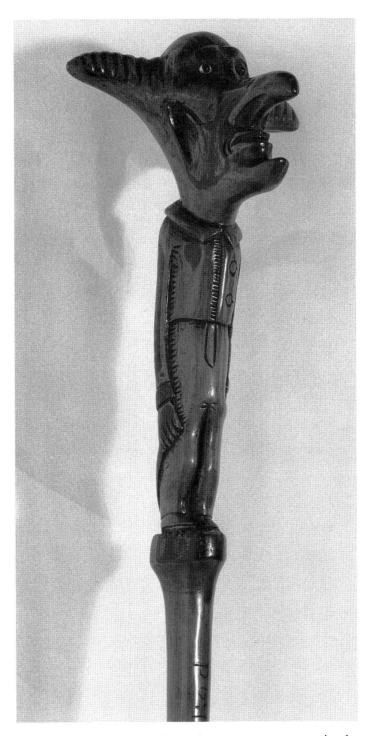

Figure 8 - A rod used in the admission of customary tenants in the manor of Church Aston, Shropshire, in the nineteenth century.

be recorded. These details need to be treated with some caution, however, as the ages given may be approximate rather than strictly accurate. Nevertheless a single account of a surrender and admission on a court roll may include information on three generations of tenants.

Manor court rolls primarily record the descent of copyhold land. However, various other land transactions were made and you may therefore come across some entries that require explanation. Customary tenants commonly had the right to let their copyhold land but often the custom of the manor decreed that they must first obtain the permission of their lord. Court rolls therefore often contain information relating to the granting of licences to customary tenants for them to let their land. A customary tenant might also sell his land and, again, the process had to be conducted by surrender and admission in the manor court.

By the eighteenth century it had become common for tenants to raise loans on their land in the form of mortgages and court rolls from this period commonly record the details of mortgages entered into by customary tenants. These entries are known as **conditional surrenders**. The tenant wishing to take out a mortgage on his land would come to the manor court and surrender the land into the hands of the steward. This would be recorded on the manor court rolls as a conditional surrender and would include the terms of the mortgage. The mortgagee would not be admitted to the holding but if the mortgagor failed to repay the mortgage debt within the specified time then the mortgagee had the right to be admitted tenant. If the tenant repaid the mortgage then the conditional surrender would be declared void and the acknowledgement of the satisfaction of the mortgage debt would be recorded on the court rolls.

For example at the court baron of the manor of Egham in 1732 a conditional surrender was made by a customary tenant, James Richardson. He took out a mortgage to the value of sixty pounds from William Johnson and his wife Elizabeth on a piece of land in Jugfield. In 1736 the court records the satisfaction of the mortgage by Richardson. The entry in the court book is a follows:-

'Whereas at a court held for this mannor the seventeenth day of October in the year 1732 James Richardson a customary tenant of this manor did surrender ALL that his customary messuage with the appurtenances scituate in Jugfield in the parish of Egham within this mannor TO THE USE AND BEHOOF of William Johnson and Elizabeth his wife their heirs and assigns for ever under condition that if the said James Richardson did pay or cause to be paid unto the said William Johnson and Elizabeth his wife their executors administrators or assigns the sum of sixty pounds with lawfull interest for the same on the twenty sixth day of December then next ensuing That then the said surrender should be void, otherwise should remain in full force and virtue. NOW AT THIS COURT came the said William Johnson in his proper person and acknowledged to have recd full satisfaction of and for the said sum of sixty pounds and all interest for the same according to the form and effect of the said surrender'.

Finally, while in theory customary land descended according to the custom of the manor, by the eighteenth century this was frequently circumvented by a device known as a **surrender to the uses of a will** whereby a tenant might leave his customary land to a chosen heir. At the Egham court used as the example above, James Richardson sold his land in Jugfield to Henry, Earl of Stirling. The court book records his surrender of the land to the steward and the admittance of the Earl as tenant by the rod. The Earl then surrendered the land back to the steward to be disposed of upon the Earl's death according to the terms of his will:

'To such uses, intents and purposes as the said Earl in and by his last will and testament in writing had directed limited or appointed or should direct limit or appoint'.

Subsidiary Court Records

As well as the court rolls and books there are a number of other types of documents which are associated with the manor court, which may contain useful information. The transactions which occurred in the manor court were noted down in draft form as the court proceeded and these records sometimes survive either in the form of draft rolls or, later, as **minute books**. These, as you might expect, are often rapidly written and less easy to read than the formal court rolls or books, but if the court rolls have not survived the minutes may serve as a substitute.

Estreat rolls were also often made. These were produced to record the details of the amercements or fines imposed by the court and the details of the heriots and entry fines to be collected. This information would be copied on to small rolls or pieces of parchment for use by the bailiff who normally had the job of collecting the fines imposed by the court. The estreat rolls often begin with a very similar opening to the court rolls and care should be taken not to confuse them with actual court rolls.

After the opening the estreat rolls simply list the names of the tenants who have been amerced and give brief details of their offences and of the amount they have to pay. *Figure 9* (LR 11/58/847F) is an estreat roll for the manor of Havering Atte Bower. It begins with a list of the tenants who have not attended the court session and who are therefore amerced 3d apiece. It then states that three tenants are amerced for causing affray and bloodshed, and two tenants Richard Perryn and Lawrence Pake

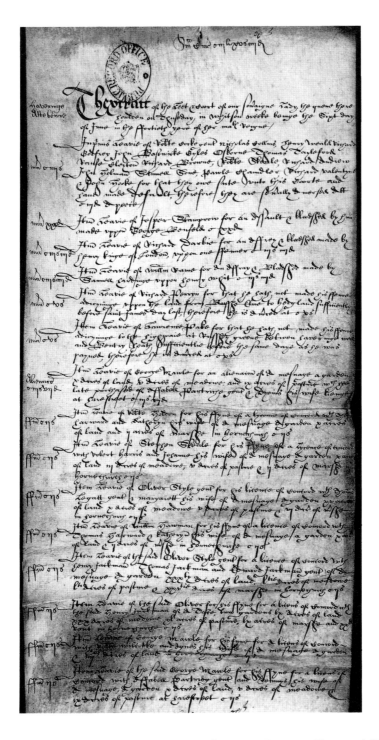

Figure 9 - Estreats for the manor of Havering atte Bower, Essex, 1598. (LR 11/58/847F)

are amerced for failing to repair their hedges. The rest of the roll is taken up with the fines levied on tenants for the grant of licences permitting them to let out their holdings.

If the lord's officials had difficulty in collecting the amercements on some manors the bailiff had the right to **distrain** or impound a tenants goods or chattels until the amercement was paid. However it is not unusual for tenants to be presented at several sessions for failing to carry out some order of the court.

On some manors it seems to have been the practice to maintain lists of tenants purely for administrative purposes. These could take the form of **suit rolls**: lists of all those who owed suit to the manor courts. Researchers will also occasionally come across **call books**. These listed the tenants who owed suit to the court but, as *figure 10* (CRES 5/469) shows, they were also used as court attendance registers. The marks against the names of the tenants indicate whether or not they attended sessions of the courts. The death of a tenant is noted in a number of cases and sometimes the name of the new tenant has been entered. Individual manorial stewards also sometimes kept **registers of surrenders and admissions** which are records of the transfers of copyhold land kept, for some reason, separately from the court rolls.

Later courts

The amount of business conducted in the manor courts declined from the eighteenth century. Increasingly, the courts were concerned exclusively with the surrender and admittance of copyhold land. As we discussed when looking at manorial tenancies, many manorial lords were keen to convert customary land to leasehold wherever possible and this meant that the amount of copyhold land was continually being reduced, to the extent that in some manors none was left. Hence there was no reason for the manor court to continue to meet. Finally, during the eighteenth and

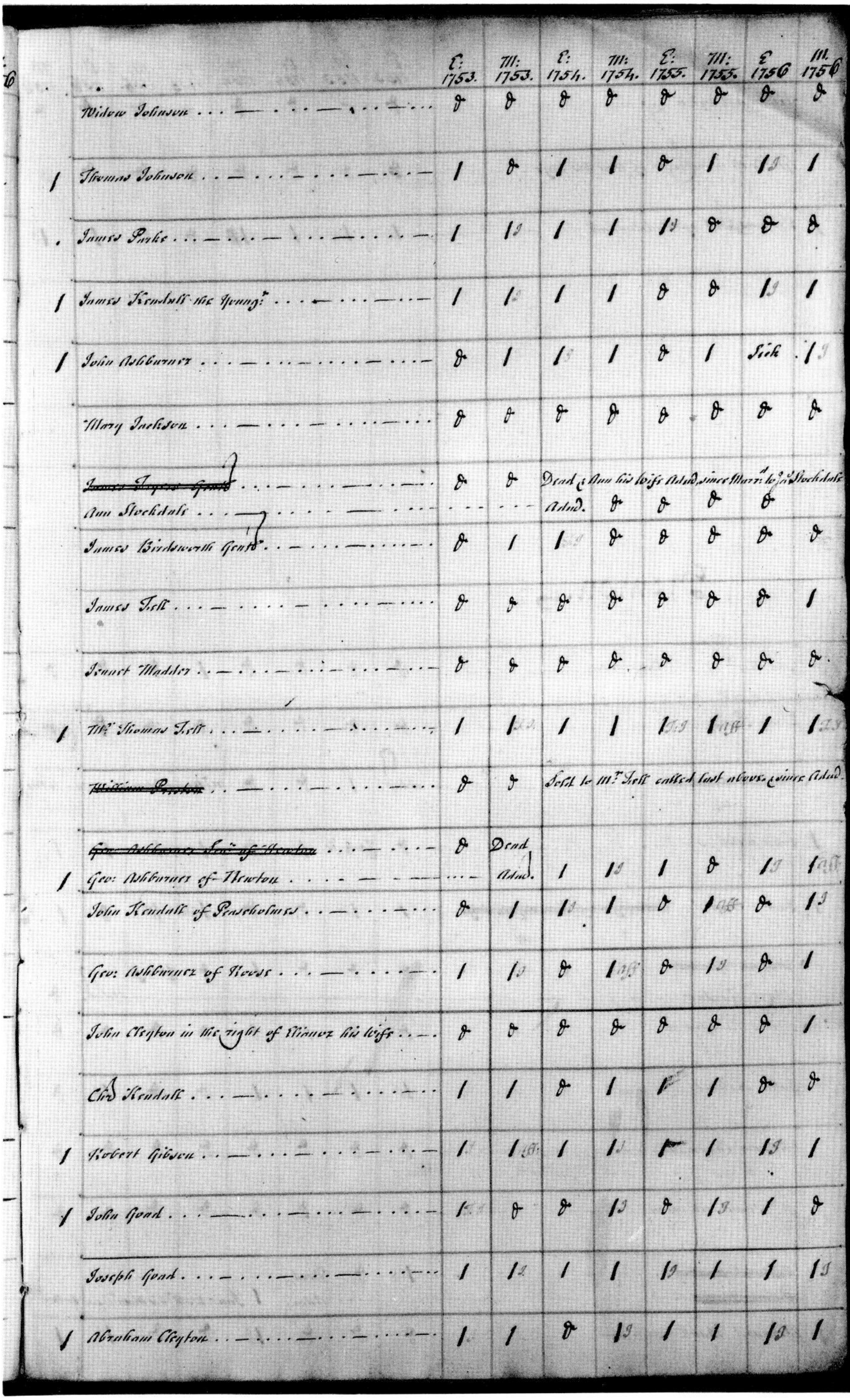

		E: 1753.	M: 1753.	E: 1754.	M: 1754.	E: 1755.	M: 1755.	E 1756	M. 1756
	Widow Johnson	0	0	0	0	0	0	0	0
/	Thomas Johnson	1	0	1	1	0	1	1s	1
	James Parke	1	1s	1	1	1s	0	0	0
/	James Kendall the Young^r	1	1	1	1	0	0	1s	1
/	John Ashburner	0	1	1	1	0	1	Sick	1
	Mary Jackson	0	0	0	0	0	0	0	0
	~~James Tyson Grant~~	0	0	Dead & Ann his wife Adm^d since Marr^d to J^no Stockdale					
	Ann Stockdale			Adm^d.	0	0	0	0	
	James Birdsworth Grant	0	1	1	0	0	0	0	0
	James Fell	0	0	0	0	0	0	0	1
	Jennet Madder	0	0	0	0	0	0	0	0
/	Mr Thomas Fell	1	1	1	1	1	1	1	1
	~~William Preston~~	0	0	Sold to Mr Fell called last above & since Adm^d.					
	~~Geo: Ashburner Senr of Newton~~	0	Dead						
/	Geo: Ashburner of Newton		Adm^d.	1	1s	1	0	1	1
	John Kendall of Peaseholmes	0	1	1	1	0	1	0	1s
	Geo: Ashburner of Rooss	1	1	0	1	0	1	0	1
	John Clayton in the right of Minor his wife	0	0	0	0	0	0	0	1
	Chr. Kendall	1	1	0	1	1	1	0	0
/	Robert Gibson	1	1	1	1	1	1	1s	1
/	John Goad	1	0	0	1s	0	1s	1	0
	Joseph Goad	1	1	1	1	1s	1	1	1s
/	Abraham Clayton	1	1	0	1s	1	1	1s	1

Figure 10 - Call book for the manor of Muchland and Torver, Lancashire, eighteenth century. (CRES 5/469)

nineteenth centuries it became increasingly common for surrenders and admissions to take place outside the meeting of the court baron. By this date, estate or manorial stewards were often local solicitors who were prepared to deal with surrenders and admissions in their own offices, although the transactions would still be recorded in the manor court book.

Enfranchisement and the Extinguishment of Manorial Incidents

By the beginning of the nineteenth century calls were being made for the abolition of copyhold tenure because it was held to be anachronistic and the procedure of admission and surrender inconvenient. Consequently, permissive legislation passed from 1841 onwards allowed for the 'enfranchisement', or conversion to freehold, of copyhold land. The process could be initiated by either lord or tenant and the other party had to agree, although the lord of the manor was entitled to compensation for the loss of his manorial incidents (such as the payment of a heriot or entry fine). Where a satisfactory agreement could not be reached between the lord and tenant, the Ministry of Agriculture could be approached to fix the level of the award of compensation.

The deeds (for voluntary arrangements) and the awards (for compulsory enfranchisement) from 1841-1925 are held by the PRO in the class **MAF 9**. They are arranged by county, manor, date, and tenants name and include evidences of title supplied by manorial lords from 1900. Evidences of title supplied from 1840 to 1900 will be found in **MAF 20** listed alphabetically by manor.

Copyhold tenure was eventually compulsorily abolished by the Law of Property Act 1922 and all remaining copyhold land was enfranchised from 1 January 1926. Some manorial incidents remained after this date but they could be extinguished by the payment of compensation to the lord by the former copyhold tenant. The class

MAF 13 contains Certificates declaring that the amount of compensation had been determined in compulsory cases, and Compensation Agreements for voluntary cases.

Under the provisions of the 1922 Act (Section 140) all remaining manorial incidents were automatically extinguished on 1 January 1936. However, for a period of five years after this date lords of manors or owners of land out of which these incidents issued had the right to apply to the Ministry of Agriculture for an award determining the amount of compensation for extinguishment. Certificates of the determination of extinguishment for the period 1 January 1936 to 28 November 1939 will be found in **MAF 27**. No applications were permitted after this date except for the period 1 November 1949 to 31 October 1950 which was appointed by Order in Council to resolve outstanding cases. Certificates of determination issued during this period will also be found in **MAF 27**. Manorial registers containing references to certificates and awards in this class and **MAF 13** are in **MAF 76**. Registered files dealing with manorial incidents are in **MAF 48** and **MAF 233**.

SELECT BIBLIOGRAPHY

Bennet, H.S., *Life on the English Manor: A Study of Peasant Conditions, 1150-1400,* Cambridge, 1960.

Farr, M.W., (ed.), *Accounts and Surveys of the Wiltshire lands of Adam de Stratton,* devizes, 1959.

Harley, J.B., *Maps for the Local Historian: A Guide to the British Sources,* London, 1972.

Harvey, P.D.A., *Manorial Records,* London, 1984.

Harvey, P.D.A., (ed.), *Manorial Records of Cuxham, Oxfordshire, circa 1200-1359,* London 1979.

Harvey, P.D.A., *Maps in Tudor England,* London, 1993.

Jacob, Giles, *The Compleat Court Keeper,* London, 1713.

Kerridge, Eric, (ed.), *Agrarian Problems in the Sixteenth Century and After,* London, 1969.

Kerridge, Eric, (ed.), 'Surveys of the Manors of Philip, First Earl of Pembroke and Montgomery 1631-2', *Wiltshire Archaeological and Natural History Society,* 1953.

Lomas, T., 'The Development of the Manorial Extent', *Journal of the Society of Archivists,* vi (1980), pp260-73.

Richardson, John, *The Local Historians Encyclopaedia,* (2nd edn.), 1986.

Simpson,A.W.B., *An Introduction to the History of the Land Law,* London, 1961.

Stratton, C.R., *Surveys of the Lands of William, First Earl of Pembroke,* 2 vols., London, 1909.

Stuart, Denis, *Manorial Records, an Introduction to their transcription and translation,* Chichester, 1992.

Travers, Anita, 'Manorial Documents', *Genealogists' Magazine,* xxi (1983), pp1-19.

West, John, *Village Records,* Chichester, 1962.

INDEX

Index references should be used in conjunction with the contents list. They refer only to the first entry in the text, where the terms are explained.

PART TWO:
Locating Manorial Records

SECTION A:

Using the Manorial Documents Register at the Royal Commission on Historical Manuscripts

Introduction

The first task of the searcher wishing to consult manorial records is to locate the records relating to the relevant manors. In most cases this should be a straightforward procedure. Large numbers of manorial records are to be found in the local record offices of the counties to which they relate and it is a relatively easy task to check the finding aids maintained by these offices to determine what manorial records they hold. Some, for example Staffordshire Record Office, have even published guides to their manorial holdings.

On the other hand, many manorial records are not to be found in the appropriate local record offices and they are frequently located far from their natural geographical homes. There are various reasons for this. Ancient institutions, such as older Oxford and Cambridge colleges, own large amounts of land spread over England and Wales and their muniment rooms contain substantial quantities of manorial records relating to these lands. The Crown too held extensive lands throughout the country and many of the manorial records deriving from the administration of Crown lands are now to be found in the PRO. Therefore, when you begin to investigate the holdings of the relevant record office it is by no means certain that you will find all of the records which are extant for your manor. Fortunately, however, it should not be too difficult to discover the whereabouts of other surviving documents because of the existence of the Manorial Documents Register (MDR).

The Manorial Documents Register

Manorial records are almost the only class of historical documents generated by private institutions and individuals which enjoy some degree of statutory protection and are subject to compulsory registration. This unique status has helped to ensure the preservation of the records in large quantities, and it has brought further benefits to the user in that surviving records for any given manor are now relatively easy to trace because their existence is noted on the MDR.

The register, which is maintained by the Historical Manuscripts Commission, is the main tool for researchers who wish to trace manorial records. It is particularly indispensable for locating records which have become dispersed and have strayed from the geographical areas to which they refer. For example, the records of the manor of Stratford-upon-Avon are split between the Public Record Office, the Shakespeare Birthplace Trust Record Office, Warwickshire County Record Office, the Centre for Kentish Studies in Maidstone, and the Folger Shakespeare Library, Washington. It is only the MDR which brings all this type of information together for all manors throughout England and Wales. The MDR does not cover the Channel Islands or Scotland.

However, before proceeding to describe the MDR and how to use it there are a number of matters which need to be considered so that, as a researcher, you can get the maximum benefit from the MDR.

The Legal Background

The Origins of the Manorial Documents Register

Noting the existence of manorial records for the benefit of researchers was not the original purpose of the MDR. In 1922 the Law of Property Act brought to an end the last meaningful function of manorial courts by abolishing the form of land tenure known as 'copyhold'. As discussed in the earlier part of this book the distinguishing feature of copyhold tenure was that any transfer in the ownership of land held by copyhold had to be conducted by the process known as 'surrender and admission' in the court of the appropriate manor. By the nineteenth century this was proving to be extremely inconvenient as it meant, for example, that freehold and copyhold land could not be conveyed in a single transaction. A series of permissive acts passed during the nineteenth century had allowed for the voluntary conversion to freehold or 'enfranchisement' of copyhold land, but the Law of Property Act finally abolished the arcane process of surrender and admission and, in one go, enfranchised all remaining copyhold land. The problem remained, however, that for many holders of former copyhold land proof of title could still depend upon the account of the surrender and subsequent admission recorded in a manor court book. It was, therefore, essential that these records should not be lost or destroyed.

To ensure their survival a further piece of legislation, the Law of Property (Amendment) Act 1924, put manorial records under the 'charge and superintendence of the Master of the Rolls', entrusting him with the responsibility to ensure that all such documents were preserved. To achieve the aims of the 1924 Act he formed a Manorial Documents Committee, based at the Public Record Office. The committee's brief was to draw up guidelines or rules to facilitate the location and preservation of manorial records, to record on a register the whereabouts of such records and to approve a network of local repositories capable of providing suitable accommodation for manorial documents should an owner or custodian wish to deposit any records in his or her possession.

The committee, by means of advertisements in the press and by writing directly to likely owners or custodians, began to compile a complete list of all the manors in England and Wales as a precursor to collecting information relating to the whereabouts of manorial records. The response to these initial approaches brought in an enormous amount of information regarding the existence of manors. More detailed information concerning manorial records was then requested on standard forms which were sent out to the owners or custodians. The returns from custodians formed the basis of the MDR, which was maintained by the PRO until 1959 when responsibility for its maintenance was transferred to the Historical Manuscripts Commission. The minutes and papers relating to the activities of the Manorial Documents Committee, along with the returns made by owners and custodians, are now preserved at the PRO, Kew in the class **HMC 5**.

The Provisions of the Manorial Documents Rules

Enshrined in the 1924 Act was a statutory right of access to original manorial records for all persons with an interest in former copyhold lands. The act did *not* establish an automatic right of access to manorial records for individuals pursuing personal research. The right to consult manorial records was reserved for those who had a legal interest in former copyhold land and who might require access to the records to prove title.

The original Manorial Documents Rules drawn up by the Manorial Documents Committee have been amended several times. Full copies can be obtained from the

Historical Manuscripts Commission but the most important provisions are now as follows:-

1.　　No manorial documents may be removed from England or Wales without the permission of the Master of the Rolls (in practice this is never granted).

2.　　Owners or custodians of manorial records are under an obligation to provide the Secretary of the Historical Manuscripts Commission with brief details of any documents in their possession for inclusion on the Manorial Documents Register. Any change in ownership of manorial records must be notified to him.

3.　　Owners or custodians are required to ensure that any manorial documents for which they are responsible are kept under safe and proper conditions.

4.　　If the Secretary of the Historical Manuscripts Commission is not satisfied with the conditions in which documents are being stored he can direct the owner to place the documents on deposit in a repository which has been approved by the Commission for this purpose. This will normally be the appropriate local record office.

Access to Manorial Records

The Historical Manuscripts Commission does not keep any manorial records itself. The vast majority of such records are now deposited in public repositories where they are available for research. A significant number, however, remain in the possession of private individuals or institutions and their existence is noted on the MDR. Some of these privately-held records may not be made available to searchers as a matter of course and, as indicated previously, searchers do not have any legal right to consult manorial records for the purposes of personal research. In other cases a charge may be levied for the use of privately-held records. The search room officer on duty at the Historical Manuscripts Commission should be able to advise searchers on the availability of such records and also provide information on how a particular private owner should be approached.

The Survival of Manorial Records

Although the Manorial Documents Rules have contributed enormously to the survival of manorial records, it is important to remember that, like many other classes of historic records, the survival rate is inevitably patchy. The loss of some records will be due to accidental destruction. The early records of the manor of Pembrey, Pembrokeshire, for example, seem to have met with a rather unfortunate end. A note among the papers of the Earls of Ashburnham in the National Library of Wales accounts for the lack of early records for this manor saying 'it is unfortunate that the early court rolls and charters referring to the manor were lost during the last century when the steward of the manor had a boating accident'.

No doubt the records of other manors will have suffered unusual but equally disastrous accidents. Others may simply have been discarded and destroyed as their owners believed that they had no further administrative use and were taking up space which could be utilized for a different purpose. Some may simply have decayed in inadequate storage conditions. For only a small proportion of manors, therefore, will there be a significant quantity of records surviving from the medieval period. It is much more likely that surviving manorial records will begin in the mid-sixteenth or seventeenth centuries, and even for these later documents searchers will be very fortunate not to find frustrating gaps in the series.

The Manorial Documents Register and Manorial Lordships

The MDR is a register of the whereabouts of manorial documents and is not a register of title to manorial lordships. Such lordships are still sold regularly by auction and by private treaty, but the purchase of a title does not bring with it, as of right, any manorial documents not specifically included in the conveyance. In numerous cases, therefore, the owner of manorial documents will now have no connection whatsoever with the current lord of the manor. This situation has arisen because of the legal case *Beaumont v Jeffrey* (1925) which established that the lord of a manor could sell the lordship while retaining ownership of any records in his possession relating to the manor. Conversely, it was also established that manorial documents could be disposed of by the lord while the lordship itself could be retained.

Unlike owners of manorial records there is no legal requirement for owners of manorial lordships to register their title and it can, therefore, be difficult to trace the descent of a title or its current owner. Some incidental information relating to the historic owners of manorial lordships is noted on the MDR but this information may well be out of date. It is mainly derived from information supplied to the Manorial Documents Committee by the Ministry of Agriculture and the Board of Inland Revenue, both of which had accumulated by 1925 a considerable amount of detail relating to the existence of manors and the ownership of manorial lordships. The Ministry of Agriculture information was mainly taken from its files under the Copyhold Acts, and the Chief Inspector of Taxes requested local tax inspectors to supply similar information to the Manorial Documents Committee. These lists of manors and owners of titles are held by the PRO under the reference HMC 5/6-8. The MDR itself is not, therefore, usually of much direct help for those who wish to trace the descent or ownership of a manorial lordship.

By far the best sources of information for tracing the descent of manors are the *Victoria History of the Counties of England (VCH)*. For those counties for which volumes of the *VCH* were compiled earlier this century there are often 'potted histories' which trace the descent of individual manors and give a great deal of other useful information regarding the manor. They may, for example, note the date at which the manor courts ceased to function.

The *VCH* should be available for consultation in the local studies section of your local library or record office. Local libraries should also hold copies of local history journals and local record society publications. It is always worth checking such printed sources for any articles or studies which relate to your particular manor, or even published transcripts or calendars of groups of manorial records. You could save a great deal of time if the ground has already been broken by a previous researcher!

Consulting the Manorial Documents Register

Now that we have considered the background to the MDR and some if its limitations we can turn to the MDR itself.

How to use the Manorial Documents Register

The MDR is a card index which is arranged by the pre-1974 'historic counties'. It is divided into two sections:

- parishes index
- manor index

The parishes index indicates which manor or manors lay within a parish (where this has been established) and is arranged alphabetically by parish. If, for example, you know that an individual held land in a particular parish but you do not know the name of the manor(s) within that parish you would need to consult the parishes index to identify the names of the manor(s). It is, of course, always important to bear in mind that manor and parish boundaries were not always coterminous. A manor could cross the boundaries of several parishes, while there could be land held of several manors within a single parish.

The manor index is arranged alphabetically by manor and provides the information relating to the surviving manorial records. This information is only intended to be brief and summary and is, therefore, confined to a description of the type of document: for example, 'custumal' or 'court book', and the date(s) of the document(s). No information is given regarding the contents of the documents or, for example, the language in which they are written. The index indicates the whereabouts of the documents described and, for documents which are held in record repositories, the call number may also be given. It is, incidentally, always worth noting down reference numbers since this information can save a great deal of time when you visit the repository concerned to consult the documents.

This is how the information appears on an MDR slip. The parish and county names are on the left hand side, the manor name on the right hand side:

Eastry			Eastry
Kent			
	minutes	1733-4, 1736-1738-9, 1744, 1752	
	court roll	1702-17	
Canterbury City and Cathedral Archives		U15/14/17	

The addresses and other details of local record offices and repositories which hold the majority of manorial records can be found in *Record Repositories in Great Britain* (9th edn., HMSO, 1992).

Computerisation of the Manorial Documents Register

Since 1994 the Historical Manuscripts Commission has been undertaking a project to upgrade and computerise the Manorial Documents Register. It is anticipated that it will take at least ten years to complete this process. Working in collaboration with the National Library of Wales, the sections relating to the thirteen old counties of Wales have been completed. The rest of the MDR will be dealt with on a county by county basis, as resources allow.

The database created includes the same information as the paper index - a description of the document(s), with details of covering date(s), the physical location of the document(s) and a call number. However, considerable efforts have been made to improve the accuracy and consistency of document descriptions. The database also offers considerable advantages over the paper index in the variety and scope of searches possible.

It is still of course possible to identify all the surviving documents for a particular manor, but the database also offers the facility to define searches further. It is possible to search for documents within a specified date range, for documents held by an individual repository, or for a particular type of document through asking the database to search for a particular keywork, or for any combination of these criteria. It is therefore possible, for example, to search for all the court rolls for the period between 1500 and 1800 which relate to the manor of Chepstow and which are held in Gwent Record Office. The database also allows broader searches across a county. For example you could ask the database to identify all sixteenth-century court rolls for manors in the county of Glamorgan held by the PRO.

It should be noted that because of the general difficulty in identifying the boundaries of Welsh manors, the database for Wales does not include any information on which manor or manors lay within individual parishes. The sections of the database dealing with English counties will identify for each manor the parish in which the demesne land lay.

Following on from the Welsh project, work is now well advanced on computerising sections relating to the three former Yorkshire ridings.

Consulting the Manorial Documents Register Database

It is possible to search the database in the search room of the Historical Manuscripts Commission. Details of opening hours are given below. On-line access to the Welsh section is also possible from the search room of the Department of Manuscripts and Records at the National Library of Wales, Aberystwyth. In addition, all the county record offices in Wales have been supplied with a print-out detailing all the surviving documents for their particular county.

Access to the database via the internet is also planned. Further information will appear on the Historical Manuscripts Commission's website. The address is **www.hmc.gov.uk**.

Search Room Information

The MDR is available for public consultation in the search room of the Historical Manuscripts Commission at Quality House, Quality Court, Chancery Lane, London

WC2A 1HP. The search room is open Monday to Friday from 9.30 am - 5 pm, except at Christmas, Easter and other public holidays. Appointments are not required and no reader's ticket is necessary, although searchers are required to sign a register daily. A map showing the location of the Historical Manuscripts Commission is appended to this section.

Postal Enquiries

For those who are unable to visit the search room in person, answers to limited and specific enquiries can be dealt with by post without charge. Postal enquirers should specify the name of the manor or parish and the relevant county in which they are interested. Stamped addressed envelopes are appreciated. Enquiries may also be sent by email. The address is **nra@hmc.gov.uk**.

The National Register of Archives

One final piece of information concerning the Historical Manuscripts Commission which is worth noting is that in addition to the MDR the Commission maintains the National Register of Archives (NRA). The NRA comprises over 40,000, mainly unpublished, catalogues describing the manuscript holdings of the network of county record offices, and also the manuscript collections of numerous private owners, businesses, and other institutions throughout the United Kingdom. Each catalogue is given an NRA number and they are filed in a numerical sequence in the Commission's search room. The inflow of these catalogues is one of the means whereby the MDR is updated, as they are always trawled for references to manorial documents. An NRA number, (for example NRA 20151), given on the reverse of an MDR slip indicates when information has been taken from an NRA catalogue. It is often worth taking the trouble to look at the relevant catalogue as it may well amplify the brief information given on the MDR.

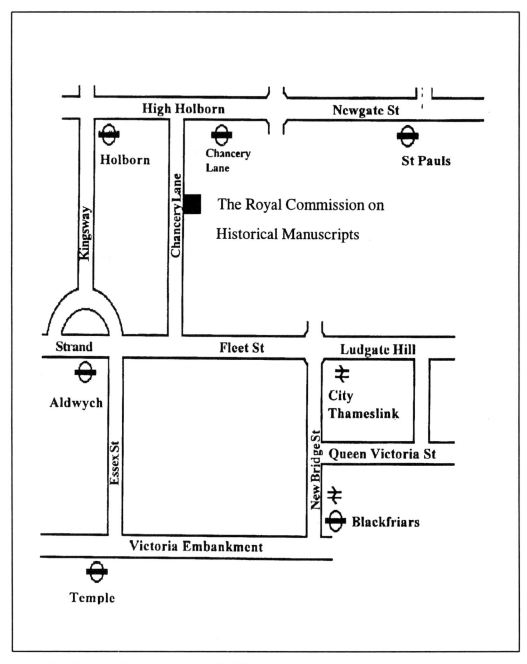

Map showing the location of the HMC.

SECTION B:

Locating Manorial Records in the Public Record Office

Introduction

The Public Record Office (PRO) contains a vast quantity of manorial documents which derive from a variety of sources. As you might expect the majority are connected with administration of the Crown's estates but there are also, for example, significant quantities of manorial records which were submitted as evidence in legal cases in Chancery and which have no connection with Crown lands. The records range in date from the medieval period to the beginning of the twentieth century and include material relating to every county in England and Wales.

Given the quantity and diversity of material in the PRO, locating documents may at first appear to be a rather daunting prospect. But researchers should not be deterred, as the PRO maintains a set of finding aids which will enable you to locate any records relevant to your manorial research. Unlike many other repositories, the PRO does not have a consolidated topographical index of its holdings. Instead manorial records in the PRO have been arranged and listed by type of document: for example, court rolls or surveys. This section of the book is intended to provide a simple guide to the finding aids and gives step by step instructions to allow you to locate and order the records that you require.

Before proceeding further there are one or two terms which are particular to the PRO and which you need to understand before you will be able to comprehend the finding aids.

All records in the PRO are divided into **classes,** reflecting, as far as possible, their original administrative arrangement. Each class is identified by a **lettercode**, for example **DL** for records produced by the **Duchy of Lancaster,** and a **class number**, for example **DL 30** for the court rolls relating to the Duchy of Lancaster's manors.

To find out more about the record classes, their administrative history and the provenance of the records contained in them you should refer to M S Giuseppi's *Guide to the Contents of the Public Record Office* (HMSO 1963, 1968) and also to the *Current Guide to the Contents of the Public Record Office*. The latter, which is available in hard copy (on site) and for sale on microfiche (PRO Publications, 1996), is the most up to date means of reference to the PRO but in some respects it has not entirely superseded Giuseppi's *Guide*. Table 1 given below does not attempt to summarize the administrative history of the manorial records in the PRO or to detail their provenance. For information of this type you should look at one or both of the guides. However, the table provides you with sufficient information to locate any manorial documents held in the PRO.

Finding Aids

Table 1 provides a detailed list of the finding aids available at the PRO. They are arranged by type of document. The left hand column indicates which record classes contain which types of manorial records by means of the lettercodes and class numbers. The right hand column indicates the finding aids which you should use for these record classes. There are two types of finding aid:

-   published volumes

-   unpublished catalogues, most of which are typed although a few are handwritten.

TABLE 1 - RECORD CLASSES AND FINDING AIDS

Court Rolls, Estreats and Presentments	Published Finding Aids
Record Classes DL 30, SC 2, E 315, DURH 3, WARD 2, E 36, SP 2, SP 14, 16, 17, 23, 28, LR 11, DL 42, SC 6, SC 12, E 137, C 54, E 306 (includes some estreats, but not copies of court rolls, which will be found amongst Deeds and Evidences).	*Volume* Lists and Indexes VI
C 103	List and Index Society 13
C 110	List and Index Society 14
ADM 74, C 104-109, C 111-116, C 171, CRES 5, DL 30/351-587, E 140, F 14, J 90, PRO 30.26, TS 19, SC 2/252-350, SC 2/506-592, LR 3, LR 11, MAF 5	**Unpublished Finding Aids** Standard or Typed Lists
New index of court rolls other than those listed in L & I VI; covering material from classes: ADM 74, C 116, CRES 5, F 14, LR 3, LR 11, MAF 5, PRO 30/26, TS 19	Union Place Name Index to Court Rolls
Ministers' Accounts DL 29, SC 6	**Published Finding Aids** Lists and Indexes V
SC 6	Lists and Indexes VIII
SC 6, DL 29, E 315, E 36	Lists and Indexes XXXIV
SC 6, DL 29	Lists and Indexes Supplementary Series, III, 1-7 (expands on part of Lists and Indexes XXXIV)
LR 7, LR 8, LR 9, (WARD 11: fragment of minister's account, unfit for production)	**Unpublished Finding Aids** Standard or Typed List
Rentals and Surveys SC 11, SC 12, DL 29, DL 42, DL 43, DL 44, SP 10 - SP 18, SP 46, E 36, E 142, E 164, E 315, E 317, LR 2	**Published Finding Aids** Lists and Indexes XXV

ADM 79, C 47/37, CRES 34, CRES 35, CRES 39, F 17, LR 13, LRRO 12, (WARD 9 - material now in SC 12), (WARD 11 - one survey, unfit for production)	**Unpublished Finding Aids** Standard or Typed Lists
Maps Various; including DL 31, LRRO 1/1-1356	**Published Finding Aids** *Maps and Plans in the Public Record Office*, I: British Isles (A complete list of classes in which maps appear is given in the Appendix. Maps included in this volume and elsewhere will usually have been given a Map Room reference number (besides its original reference) and it is this Map Room reference which should be used when ordering documents)
LRRO 1/1357-5141	**Unpublished Finding Aids** Standard or Typed Lists
Enfranchisement MAF 9, MAF 13, MAF 20, MAF 27, MAF 48, MAF 76, MAF 233	**Unpublished Finding Aids** Standard Lists
Various PEV 1, WALE 15	**Published Finding Aids** Lists and Indexes XL
DL 28, DL 31, DL 32, DL 41, DL 42	Lists and Indexes XIV
DL 28, DL 30, DL 41, DL 43, DL 44, DL 50	Lists and Indexes Supplementary Series V no 1
WARD 2 (material other than court rolls in L & I VI)	**Unpublished Finding Aids** Deputy Keeper's 6th Report (1845) Appendix II; printed, annotated and used as list
C 154	Deputy Keeper's 5th Report Appendix II
CRES 2, LR 9, LRRO 5, LRRO 11, LRRO 37, LRRO 67	Standard or Typed Lists

Using the Finding Aids

When you have located the documents you wish to consult from either a published or unpublished finding aid your next task will be to compile a full document reference so that you can order the document.

A full document reference consists of three elements:

- the lettercode
- the class number
- the piece number which relates to the individual document.

The finding aids at the PRO have been compiled over a long period of time and, therefore, vary greatly in format. However, the majority of lists relating to manorial documents are either in the format of the published Lists and Indexes series volumes, or the modern "standard" class lists, which conform to a uniform pattern, some of which are indexed or arranged alphabetically by county. In both these types of list, the lettercode and class number usually appear at the top of the page. The third element of the reference, the piece number, usually appears in the left hand column of each page, against which is written the description of the document and a date. You can identify the piece that you require from the description and you can then note down the three elements of the reference: lettercode, class number and piece number.

Inside the front cover of some finding aids, extra help with compiling references can be found in the form of a label with an example of a reference. This may be used as a guide, but do not copy it word for word; it is only an example to show you how a full reference for that type of document should appear. One of these labels is shown overleaf:

```
┌─────────────────────────────────────────────────────┐
│ ┌───────────────────────────────────────────────────┐ │
│ │      To order a document from this list,          │ │
│ │          you will need to note                    │ │
│ │                                                   │ │
│ │                                                   │ │
│ │   lettercode &              ie      SC 2          │ │
│ │   class number                                    │ │
│ │                                                   │ │
│ │                                                   │ │
│ │   piece number             eg      153/1          │ │
│ │   (for first item in list)                        │ │
│ └───────────────────────────────────────────────────┘ │
└─────────────────────────────────────────────────────┘
```

```
┌─────────────────────────────────────────────────────┐
│ ┌───────────────────────────────────────────────────┐ │
│ │          Additional Information                   │ │
│ │                                                   │ │
│ │   See page 130 for beginning of SC 2 list         │ │
│ └───────────────────────────────────────────────────┘ │
└─────────────────────────────────────────────────────┘
```

An extract taken from a Standard List is shown below as an example of what you should expect from a finding aid of this type:

This margin not to be used	Reference CRES 5	Date	Description	CRES 5
		HAMPTON COURT, MIDDX		
		Court Books - contd		
	283	1809 Apr 20- 1819 Apr 19	No 15	Volume
	284	1819 Apr 15- 1822 Oct 21	No 16	Volume
	285	1823 Apr 17- 1827 Apr 10	No 17	Volume
	286	1827 Apr 26- 1834 Oct 16	No 18	Volume
	287	1835 Apr 30- 1840 Oct 15	No 19	Volume

For the court books in this list the record class (ie the lettercode and class number) is **CRES 5**. The piece number for the court book for 1823-1827 is **285**. The full document reference is, therefore, **CRES 5/285**.

An extract from a published List and Indexes volume is shown below as an example of what you should expect from a finding aid of this type.

		GENERAL SERIES.				
S.C.2						
Port-folio.	No.	Lands.	County.	Date.	Description of Courts, &c.	Membrane or Sheets.
153	1	Ampthill Honor, viz.:—	Bedford -	36 Hen. VIII. to 1 Edw. VI. -	Courts, Honor, and General Courts.	5
		Redbornestoke Hundred, with—	,,			
		Marston Moretaine -	,,			
		Wootton - - -	,,			
		Houghton - - -	,,			
		Maulden - - -	,,			
		Flitwick - - -	,,			
		Steppingley - -	,,			
		Ridgmont (Rugemound), with Segenhoe.	,,			
		West Cotton - -	,,			
		Lidlington (Lytlyngton) -	,,			
		Cranfield - - -	,,			
		Manshead Hundred, with—	,,			
		Eversholt - - -	,,			
		Milton - - -	,,			
		Chalgrave - - -	,,			
		Harlington - -	,,			
		Tingrith (Tyngryd) -	,,			
		Husborn Crawley - -	,,			
		Hern (Harne) - -	,,			
		Wixamtree (Wryxantree) Hundred, with—	,,			
		Warden - - -	,,			
		Barford Hundred, with—	,,			
		Colmworth - - -	,,			
		Willey Hundred, with—	,,			
		Paddington - - -	,,			
		Flitt (Fleete) Hundred, with—	,,			
		Clophill with Cainhoe (Keynho).	,,			
		Barton-in-the-Clay - -	,,			
		Pulloxhill - - -	,,			
		Shitlington - - -	,,			
		Newport Pagnell Three Hundreds, viz., Dunscowe, Moulsoe, and Seglowe, with—	Buckingham			
		Wavendon - - -	,,			

For the records in this list the record class (ie the lettercode and class number) is **SC 2**. The piece number is **153/1**. The full document reference is, therefore, **SC 2/153/1**.

Dates

As you will see from this example, many dates will be expressed as regnal years: for example, 36 Hen VIII to 1 Ed VI. This means that the period covered by the document is from the 36th year of the reign of King Henry VIII, to the 1st year of the reign of King Edward VI. Use the tables of regnal years in the Appendix to convert this into the modern format: 36 Hen VIII ran from 1544 to 1545, and 1 Ed VI ran from 1547 to 1548. Therefore the document covers 1544/5 to 1547/8. If you already know the year you require, the tables will enable you to recognise the right date in the list: for example, 1663 = 15 Charles II.

Ordering Documents

Finding a Seat

Go to the main reading room, known as the Langdale Room and ask the staff at the distribution counter for a seat. They will allocate you a seat number and a bleeper. The bleeper will be used to let you know when the documents you have ordered are ready. The bleeper will work anywhere in the building, but please make sure you return it before leaving.

Locating the Finding Aids

Sets of the finding aids will be found in the Research Enquiries Room or in the Lobby. Each set runs in alphanumeric order of lettercodes and class numbers, from **AB 1** to **ZSPC 11**.

Research Enquiries Room (as at March 1997)

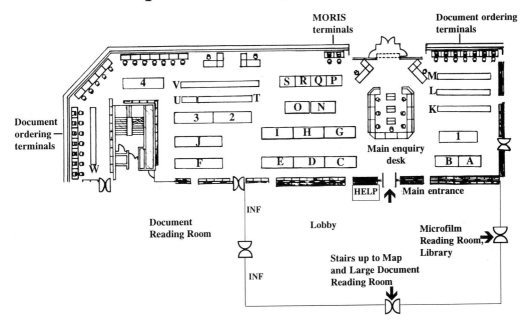

Perimeter Shelving

Standard Class Lists, PRO Guide and published works

Research Enquiries Room Tables

A-B   DO 3 and Additional Finding-Aids

C-E   T2

F   BT 32, BT 127, HO 184, IR 1, IR 17, ZPER 139

G-H   T 2 and T 3

I   T 2 and T 108

J   CO 351, CO 368, CO 372, CO 682, CO 694, CO 746, CO 763 and FO 566

K-M   Additional Finding-Aids

N-Q   ADM 12

R-S   ADM 12 and ADM 29, 139, 188 and 196

T   Printed Indexes to Foreign Office General Correspondence

U   FO 378

V   Sets of Calendars (SP, CO, T, etc.)

W   Standard (Class) Lists - Set 2

Card Indexes *

1   Drawers 1-288
2   Drawers 289-600
3   Drawers 601-912
4   Drawers 913-1194

* For contents of card index drawers, search on MORIS using title and/or class fields.

INF   Information leaflets

HELP Help Desk for initial general enquiries

NB. The location of particular finding-aids is subject to change.

MORIS

MORIS stands for Means of Reference Information System. It provides information about the locations of those finding aids and reference works which are made available for researchers in the public reading rooms at Kew and in the central London microfilm reading room. It also covers those finding aids and reference works which were formerly provided in the public reading rooms but moved to the PRO library at Kew during 1996. It does not however cover the other holdings of the PRO library, which is now open to the public. MORIS terminals in the Research Enquiries Room are located on the plan on page 93. The database can be searched by record class number, (e.g. SC 2), by title of book, or by author. Simple step-by-step instructions are given on the screen. Screen 1 reproduced below shows what you would see if you type in SC 2, reproducing the first entry on screen (as at March 1997) and also the entry for *Lists and Indexes VI.*

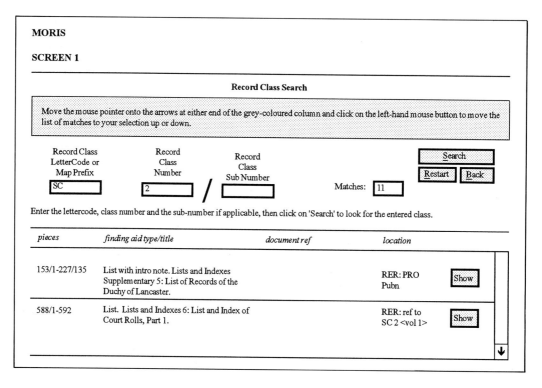

To see further information about a particular finding aid or reference work, including its location on site, use the mouse button to select show . This will bring up a second screen showing where you have to go to look at it. In this example, for SC 2, it shows that *Lists and Indexes VI* can be seen in the Research Enquiries Room and that it is shelved into the Additional Finding Aids, sometimes described as "Non-Standard class lists and Finding Aids".

MORIS

SCREEN 2

This form shows the actual location of the chosen piece. Note down the location and click on 'Back' to return to the previous screen.

Location: RER: ref in SC 2 <vol 1>

Restart   Back

Title:

Lists & Indexes 6: List and Index of Court Rolls, Part 1 (Public Record Office, 1896).

OTHER copies are held in

Building	Kew
Room	Research Enquiries Room
Location category	Additional Finding Aids
Classification Mark	
Label	ref to SC 2 <vol 1>
Classes Covered	SC 2, DL 30 & c.
Finding Aid Type	class list + index to finding aid
Document Reference	

Where to Order Documents

The documents should be ordered using one of the computer terminals in the Research Enquiries Room or on the terminal in the Map and Large Document Reading Room which is on the second floor. At the computer terminal, simply slide your reader's ticket through the bar-code reader and follow the instructions which appear on the screen. **Only three documents may be ordered at any one time**. When these are ready for collection, your bleeper will sound and you may fetch the documents from the distribution counter in the Langdale Room. You may then order three more documents and for each document you return after use, you may order one more document. All documents must be returned to the distribution counter when no longer required.

Further Information

The PRO has produced a series of information leaflets which are available free of charge on site.

Appendix-Table of Regnal Years from Henry II to William IV(1154-1837)

HENRY II

1	19 Dec. 1154–18 Dec. 1155
2	19 Dec. 1155–18 Dec. 1156
3	19 Dec. 1156–18 Dec. 1157
4	19 Dec. 1157–18 Dec. 1158
5	19 Dec. 1158–18 Dec. 1159
6	19 Dec. 1159–18 Dec. 1160
7	19 Dec. 1160–18 Dec. 1161
8	19 Dec. 1161–18 Dec. 1162
9	19 Dec. 1162–18 Dec. 1163
10	19 Dec. 1163–18 Dec. 1164
11	19 Dec. 1164–18 Dec. 1165
12	19 Dec. 1165–18 Dec. 1166
13	19 Dec. 1166–18 Dec. 1167
14	19 Dec. 1167–18 Dec. 1168
15	19 Dec. 1168–18 Dec. 1169
16	19 Dec. 1169–18 Dec. 1170
17	19 Dec. 1170–18 Dec. 1171
18	19 Dec. 1171–18 Dec. 1172
19	19 Dec. 1172–18 Dec. 1173
20	19 Dec. 1173–18 Dec. 1174
21	19 Dec. 1174–18 Dec. 1175
22	19 Dec. 1175–18 Dec. 1176
23	19 Dec. 1176–18 Dec. 1177
24	19 Dec. 1177–18 Dec. 1178
25	19 Dec. 1178–18 Dec. 1179
26	19 Dec. 1179–18 Dec. 1180
27	19 Dec. 1180–18 Dec. 1181
28	19 Dec. 1181–18 Dec. 1182
29	19 Dec. 1182–18 Dec. 1183
30	19 Dec. 1183–18 Dec. 1184
31	19 Dec. 1184–18 Dec. 1185
32	19 Dec. 1185–18 Dec. 1186
33	19 Dec. 1186–18 Dec. 1187
34	19 Dec. 1187–18 Dec. 1188
35	19 Dec. 1188–6 July 1189

RICHARD I

1	3 Sep. 1189–2 Sep. 1190
2	3 Sep. 1190–2 Sep. 1191
3	3 Sep. 1191–2 Sep. 1192
4	3 Sep. 1192–2 Sep. 1193
5	3 Sep. 1193–2 Sep. 1194
6	3 Sep. 1194–2 Sep. 1195
7	3 Sep. 1195–2 Sep. 1196
8	3 Sep. 1196–2 Sep. 1197
9	3 Sep. 1197–2 Sep. 1198
10	3 Sep. 1198–6 Apr. 1199

JOHN

1	27 May 1199–17 May 1200
2	18 May 1200–2 May 1201
3	3 May 1201–22 May 1202
4	23 May 1202–14 May 1203
5	15 May 1203–2 June 1204
6	3 June 1204–18 May 1205
7	19 May 1205–10 May 1206
8	11 May 1206–30 May 1207
9	31 May 1207–14 May 1208
10	15 May 1208–6 May 1209
11	7 May 1209–26 May 1210
12	27 May 1210–11 May 1211
13	12 May 1211–2 May 1212
14	3 May 1212–22 May 1213
15	23 May 1213–7 May 1214
16	8 May 1214–27 May 1215
17	28 May 1215–18 May 1216
18	19 May 1216–19 Oct. 1216

HENRY III

1	28 Oct. 1216–27 Oct. 1217
2	28 Oct. 1217–27 Oct. 1218
3	28 Oct. 1218–27 Oct. 1219
4	28 Oct. 1219–27 Oct. 1220
5	28 Oct. 1220–27 Oct. 1221
6	28 Oct. 1221–27 Oct. 1222
7	28 Oct. 1222–27 Oct. 1223
8	28 Oct. 1223–27 Oct. 1224
9	28 Oct. 1224–27 Oct. 1225
10	28 Oct. 1225–27 Oct. 1226
11	28 Oct. 1226–27 Oct. 1227
12	28 Oct. 1227–27 Oct. 1228
13	28 Oct. 1228–27 Oct. 1229
14	28 Oct. 1229–27 Oct. 1230
15	28 Oct. 1230–27 Oct. 1231
16	28 Oct. 1231–27 Oct. 1232
17	28 Oct. 1232–27 Oct. 1233
18	28 Oct. 1233–27 Oct. 1234
19	28 Oct. 1234–27 Oct. 1235
20	28 Oct. 1235–27 Oct. 1236
21	28 Oct. 1236–27 Oct. 1237
22	28 Oct. 1237–27 Oct. 1238
23	28 Oct. 1238–27 Oct. 1239
24	28 Oct. 1239–27 Oct. 1240
25	28 Oct. 1240–27 Oct. 1241
26	28 Oct. 1241–27 Oct. 1242
27	28 Oct. 1242–27 Oct. 1243
28	28 Oct. 1243–27 Oct. 1244
29	28 Oct. 1244–27 Oct. 1245

HENRY III–continued

30	28 Oct. 1245–27 Oct. 1246
31	28 Oct. 1246–27 Oct. 1247
32	28 Oct. 1247–27 Oct. 1248
33	28 Oct. 1248–27 Oct. 1249
34	28 Oct. 1249–27 Oct. 1250
35	28 Oct. 1250–27 Oct. 1251
36	28 Oct. 1251–27 Oct. 1252
37	28 Oct. 1252–27 Oct. 1253
38	28 Oct. 1253–27 Oct. 1254
39	28 Oct. 1254–27 Oct. 1255
40	28 Oct. 1255–27 Oct. 1256
41	28 Oct. 1256–27 Oct. 1257
42	28 Oct. 1257–27 Oct. 1258
43	28 Oct. 1258–27 Oct. 1259
44	28 Oct. 1259–27 Oct. 1260
45	28 Oct. 1260–27 Oct. 1261
46	28 Oct. 1261–27 Oct. 1262
47	28 Oct. 1262–27 Oct. 1263
48	28 Oct. 1263–27 Oct. 1264
49	28 Oct. 1264–27 Oct. 1265
50	28 Oct. 1265–27 Oct. 1266
51	28 Oct. 1266–27 Oct. 1267
52	28 Oct. 1267–27 Oct. 1268
53	28 Oct. 1268–27 Oct. 1269
54	28 Oct. 1269–27 Oct. 1270
55	28 Oct. 1270–27 Oct. 1271
56	28 Oct. 1271–27 Oct. 1272
57	28 Oct. 1272–16 Nov. 1272

EDWARD I

1	20 Nov. 1272–19 Nov. 1273
2	20 Nov. 1273–19 Nov. 1274
3	20 Nov. 1274–19 Nov. 1275
4	20 Nov. 1275–19 Nov. 1276
5	20 Nov. 1276–19 Nov. 1277
6	20 Nov. 1277–19 Nov. 1278
7	20 Nov. 1278–19 Nov. 1279
8	20 Nov. 1279–19 Nov. 1280
9	20 Nov. 1280–19 Nov. 1281
10	20 Nov. 1281–19 Nov. 1282
11	20 Nov. 1282–19 Nov. 1283
12	20 Nov. 1283–19 Nov. 1284
13	20 Nov. 1284–19 Nov. 1285
14	20 Nov. 1285–19 Nov. 1286
15	20 Nov. 1286–19 Nov. 1287
16	20 Nov. 1287–19 Nov. 1288
17	20 Nov. 1288–19 Nov. 1289
18	20 Nov. 1289–19 Nov. 1290

EDWARD I–cont.

19	20 Nov. 1290–19 Nov. 1291
20	20 Nov. 1291–19 Nov. 1292
21	20 Nov. 1292–19 Nov. 1293
22	20 Nov. 1293–19 Nov. 1294
23	20 Nov. 1294–19 Nov. 1295
24	20 Nov. 1295–19 Nov. 1296
25	20 Nov. 1296–19 Nov. 1297
26	20 Nov. 1297–19 Nov. 1298
27	20 Nov. 1298–19 Nov. 1299
28	20 Nov. 1299–19 Nov. 1300
29	20 Nov. 1300–19 Nov. 1301
30	20 Nov. 1301–19 Nov. 1302
31	20 Nov. 1302–19 Nov. 1303
32	20 Nov. 1303–19 Nov. 1304
33	20 Nov. 1304–19 Nov. 1305
34	20 Nov. 1305–19 Nov. 1306
35	20 Nov. 1306–7 July 1307

EDWARD II

1	8 July 1307–7 July 1308
2	8 July 1308–7 July 1309
3	8 July 1309–7 July 1310
4	8 July 1310–7 July 1311
5	8 July 1311–7 July 1312
6	8 July 1312–7 July 1313
7	8 July 1313–7 July 1314
8	8 July 1314–7 July 1315
9	8 July 1315–7 July 1316
10	8 July 1316–7 July 1317
11	8 July 1317–7 July 1318
12	8 July 1318–7 July 1319
13	8 July 1319–7 July 1320
14	8 July 1320–7 July 1321
15	8 July 1321–7 July 1322
16	8 July 1322–7 July 1323
17	8 July 1323–7 July 1324
18	8 July 1324–7 July 1325
19	8 July 1325–7 July 1326
20	8 July 1326–20 Jan. 1327

EDWARD III

1	25 Jan. 1327–24 Jan. 1328
2	25 Jan. 1328–24 Jan. 1329
3	25 Jan. 1329–24 Jan. 1330
4	25 Jan. 1330–24 Jan. 1331
5	25 Jan. 1331–24 Jan. 1332
6	25 Jan. 1332–24 Jan. 1333
7	25 Jan. 1333–24 Jan. 1334
8	25 Jan. 1334–24 Jan. 1335

EDWARD III–cont.

9		25 Jan. 1335–24 Jan. 1336
10		25 Jan. 1336–24 Jan. 1337
11		25 Jan. 1337–24 Jan. 1338
12		25 Jan. 1338–24 Jan. 1339
13		25 Jan. 1339–24 Jan. 1340
14	(F.1)[1]	25 Jan. 1340–24 Jan. 1341
15	(F.2)	25 Jan. 1341–24 Jan. 1342
16	(F.3)	25 Jan. 1342–24 Jan. 1343
17	(F.4)	25 Jan. 1343–24 Jan. 1344
18	(F.5)	25 Jan. 1344–24 Jan. 1345
19	(F.6)	25 Jan. 1345–24 Jan. 1346
20	(F.7)	25 Jan. 1346–24 Jan. 1347
21	(F.8)	25 Jan. 1347–24 Jan. 1348
22	(F.9)	25 Jan. 1348–24 Jan. 1349
23	(F.10)	25 Jan. 1349–24 Jan. 1350
24	(F.11)	25 Jan. 1350–24 Jan. 1351
25	(F.12)	25 Jan. 1351–24 Jan. 1352
26	(F.13)	25 Jan. 1352–24 Jan. 1353
27	(F.14)	25 Jan. 1353–24 Jan. 1354
28	(F.15)	25 Jan. 1354–24 Jan. 1355
29	(F.16)	25 Jan. 1355–24 Jan. 1356
30	(F.17)	25 Jan. 1356–24 Jan. 1357
31	(F.18)	25 Jan. 1357–24 Jan. 1358
32	(F.19)	25 Jan. 1358–24 Jan. 1359
33	(F.20)	25 Jan. 1359–24 Jan. 1360
34	(F.21)[1]	25 Jan. 1360–24 Jan. 1361
35		25 Jan. 1361–24 Jan. 1362
36		25 Jan. 1362–24 Jan. 1363
37		25 Jan. 1363–24 Jan. 1364
38		25 Jan. 1364–24 Jan. 1365
39		25 Jan. 1365–24 Jan. 1366
40		25 Jan. 1366–24 Jan. 1367
41		25 Jan. 1367–24 Jan. 1368
42		25 Jan. 1368–24 Jan. 1369
43	(F.30)	25 Jan. 1369–24 Jan. 1370
44	(F.31)	25 Jan. 1370–24 Jan. 1371
45	(F.32)	25 Jan. 1371–24 Jan. 1372
46	(F.33)	25 Jan. 1372–24 Jan. 1373
47	(F.34)	25 Jan. 1373–24 Jan. 1374
48	(F.35)	25 Jan. 1374–24 Jan. 1375
49	(F.36)	25 Jan. 1375–24 Jan. 1376
50	(F.37)	25 Jan. 1376–24 Jan. 1377
51	(F.38)	25 Jan. 1377–21 June 1377

RICHARD II

1	22 June 1377–21 June 1378
2	22 June 1378–21 June 1379
3	22 June 1379–21 June 1380
4	22 June 1380–21 June 1381
5	22 June 1381–21 June 1382
6	22 June 1382–21 June 1383
7	22 June 1383–21 June 1384

RICHARD II–cont.

8	22 June 1384–21 June 1385
9	22 June 1385–21 June 1386
10	22 June 1386–21 June 1387
11	22 June 1387–21 June 1388
12	22 June 1388–21 June 1389
13	22 June 1389–21 June 1390
14	22 June 1390–21 June 1391
15	22 June 1391–21 June 1392
16	22 June 1392–21 June 1393
17	22 June 1393–21 June 1394
18	22 June 1394–21 June 1395
19	22 June 1395–21 June 1396
20	22 June 1396–21 June 1397
21	22 June 1397–21 June 1398
22	22 June 1398–21 June 1399
23	22 June 1399–29 Sep. 1399

HENRY IV

1	30 Sep. 1399–29 Sep. 1400
2	30 Sep. 1400–29 Sep. 1401
3	30 Sep. 1401–29 Sep. 1402
4	30 Sep. 1402–29 Sep. 1403
5	30 Sep. 1403–29 Sep. 1404
6	30 Sep. 1404–29 Sep. 1405
7	30 Sep. 1405–29 Sep. 1406
8	30 Sep. 1406–29 Sep. 1407
9	30 Sep. 1407–29 Sep. 1408
10	30 Sep. 1408–29 Sep. 1409
11	30 Sep. 1409–29 Sep. 1410
12	30 Sep. 1410–29 Sep. 1411
13	30 Sep. 1411–29 Sep. 1412
14	30 Sep. 1412–20 March 1413

HENRY V

1	21 March 1413–20 March 1414
2	21 March 1414–20 March 1415
3	21 March 1415–20 March 1416
4	21 March 1416–20 March 1417
5	21 March 1417–20 March 1418
6	21 March 1418–20 March 1419
7	21 March 1419–20 March 1420
8	21 March 1420–20 March 1421
9	21 March 1421–20 March 1422
10	21 March 1422–31 Aug. 1422

HENRY VI

1	1 Sep. 1422–31 Aug. 1423
2	1 Sep. 1423–31 Aug. 1424
3	1 Sep. 1424–31 Aug. 1425
4	1 Sep. 1425–31 Aug. 1426
5	1 Sep. 1426–31 Aug. 1427
6	1 Sep. 1427–31 Aug. 1428
7	1 Sep. 1428–31 Aug. 1429
8	1 Sep. 1429–31 Aug. 1430
9	1 Sep. 1430–31 Aug. 1431
10	1 Sep. 1431–31 Aug. 1432
11	1 Sep. 1432–31 Aug. 1433
12	1 Sep. 1433–31 Aug. 1434
13	1 Sep. 1434–31 Aug. 1435
14	1 Sep. 1435–31 Aug. 1436
15	1 Sep. 1436–31 Aug. 1437
16	1 Sep. 1437–31 Aug. 1438
17	1 Sep. 1438–31 Aug. 1439
18	1 Sep. 1439–31 Aug. 1440
19	1 Sep. 1440–31 Aug. 1441
20	1 Sep. 1441–31 Aug. 1442
21	1 Sep. 1442–31 Aug. 1443
22	1 Sep. 1443–31 Aug. 1444
23	1 Sep. 1444–31 Aug. 1445
24	1 Sep. 1445–31 Aug. 1446
25	1 Sep. 1446–31 Aug. 1447
26	1 Sep. 1447–31 Aug. 1448
27	1 Sep. 1448–31 Aug. 1449
28	1 Sep. 1449–31 Aug. 1450
29	1 Sep. 1450–31 Aug. 1451
30	1 Sep. 1451–31 Aug. 1452
31	1 Sep. 1452–31 Aug. 1453
32	1 Sep. 1453–31 Aug. 1454
33	1 Sep. 1454–31 Aug. 1455
34	1 Sep. 1455–31 Aug. 1456
35	1 Sep. 1456–31 Aug. 1457
36	1 Sep. 1457–31 Aug. 1458
37	1 Sep. 1458–31 Aug. 1459
38	1 Sep. 1459–31 Aug. 1460
39	1 Sep. 1460–4 Mar. 1461
	and
49	Sep.-Oct. 1470–11 Apr. 1471

EDWARD IV

1	4 March 1461–3 March 1462
2	4 March 1462–3 March 1463
3	4 March 1463–3 March 1464
4	4 March 1464–3 March 1465
5	4 March 1465–3 March 1466
6	4 March 1466–3 March 1467
7	4 March 1467–3 March 1468
8	4 March 1468–3 March 1469
9	4 March 1469–3 March 1470
10	4 March 1470–3 March 1471
11	4 March 1471–3 March 1472
12	4 March 1472–3 March 1473

EDWARD IV-cont.

13	4 March 1473–3 March 1474
14	4 March 1474–3 March 1475
15	4 March 1475–3 March 1476
16	4 March 1476–3 March 1477
17	4 March 1477–3 March 1478
18	4 March 1478–3 March 1479
19	4 March 1479–3 March 1480
20	4 March 1480–3 March 1481
21	4 March 1481–3 March 1482
22	4 March 1482–3 March 1483
23	4 March 1483–9 April 1483

EDWARD V

1	9 April 1483–25 June 1483

RICHARD III

1	26 June 1483–25 June 1484
2	26 June 1484–25 June 1485
3	26 June 1485–22 Aug. 1485

HENRY VII

1	22 Aug. 1485–21 Aug. 1486
2	22 Aug. 1486–21 Aug. 1487
3	22 Aug. 1487–21 Aug. 1488
4	22 Aug. 1488–21 Aug. 1489
5	22 Aug. 1489–21 Aug. 1490
6	22 Aug. 1490–21 Aug. 1491
7	22 Aug. 1491–21 Aug. 1492
8	22 Aug. 1492–21 Aug. 1493
9	22 Aug. 1493–21 Aug. 1494
10	22 Aug. 1494–21 Aug. 1495
11	22 Aug. 1495–21 Aug. 1496
12	22 Aug. 1496–21 Aug. 1497
13	22 Aug. 1497–21 Aug. 1498
14	22 Aug. 1498–21 Aug. 1499
15	22 Aug. 1499–21 Aug. 1500
16	22 Aug. 1500–21 Aug. 1501
17	22 Aug. 1501–21 Aug. 1502
18	22 Aug. 1502–21 Aug. 1503
19	22 Aug. 1503–21 Aug. 1504
20	22 Aug. 1504–21 Aug. 1505
21	22 Aug. 1505–21 Aug. 1506
22	22 Aug. 1506–21 Aug. 1507
23	22 Aug. 1507–21 Aug. 1508
24	22 Aug. 1508–21 Apr. 1509

HENRY VIII

1	22 Apr. 1509–21 Apr. 1510
2	22 Apr. 1510–21 Apr. 1511
3	22 Apr. 1511–21 Apr. 1512
4	22 Apr. 1512–21 Apr. 1513
5	22 Apr. 1513–21 Apr. 1514
6	22 Apr. 1514–21 Apr. 1515
7	22 Apr. 1515–21 Apr. 1516
8	22 Apr. 1516–21 Apr. 1517
9	22 Apr. 1517–21 Apr. 1518
10	22 Apr. 1518–21 Apr. 1519
11	22 Apr. 1519–21 Apr. 1520
12	22 Apr. 1520–21 Apr. 1521
13	22 Apr. 1521–21 Apr. 1522
14	22 Apr. 1522–21 Apr. 1523
15	22 Apr. 1523–21 Apr. 1524
16	22 Apr. 1524–21 Apr. 1525
17	22 Apr. 1525–21 Apr. 1526
18	22 Apr. 1526–21 Apr. 1527
19	22 Apr. 1527–21 Apr. 1528
20	22 Apr. 1528–21 Apr. 1529
21	22 Apr. 1529–21 Apr. 1530
22	22 Apr. 1530–21 Apr. 1531
23	22 Apr. 1531–21 Apr. 1532
24	22 Apr. 1532–21 Apr. 1533
25	22 Apr. 1533–21 Apr. 1534
26	22 Apr. 1534–21 Apr. 1535
27	22 Apr. 1535–21 Apr. 1536
28	22 Apr. 1536–21 Apr. 1537
29	22 Apr. 1537–21 Apr. 1538
30	22 Apr. 1538–21 Apr. 1539
31	22 Apr. 1539–21 Apr. 1540
32	22 Apr. 1540–21 Apr. 1541
33	22 Apr. 1541–21 Apr. 1542
34	22 Apr. 1542–21 Apr. 1543
35	22 Apr. 1543–21 Apr. 1544
36	22 Apr. 1544–21 Apr. 1545
37	22 Apr. 1545–21 Apr. 1546
38	22 Apr. 1546–28 Jan. 1547

EDWARD VI

1	28 Jan. 1547–27 Jan. 1548
2	28 Jan. 1548–27 Jan. 1549
3	28 Jan. 1549–27 Jan. 1550
4	28 Jan. 1550–27 Jan. 1551
5	28 Jan. 1551–27 Jan. 1552
6	28 Jan. 1552–27 Jan. 1553
7	28 Jan. 1553–6 July 1553

JANE

1	6 July 1553–19 July 1553

MARY

1	19 July 1553–5 July 1554
2	6 July 1554 [1]–24 July 1554

PHILIP and MARY

1 & 2	25 July 1554–5 July 1555
1 & 3	6 July 1555–24 July 1555
2 & 3	25 July 1555–5 July 1556
2 & 4	6 July 1556–24 July 1556
3 & 4	25 July 1556–5 July 1557
3 & 5	6 July 1557–24 July 1557
4 & 5	25 July 1557–5 July 1558
4 & 6	6 July 1558–24 July 1558
5 & 6	25 July 1558–17 Nov. 1558

ELIZABETH I

1	17 Nov. 1558–16 Nov. 1559
2	17 Nov. 1559–16 Nov. 1560
3	17 Nov. 1560–16 Nov. 1561
4	17 Nov. 1561–16 Nov. 1562
5	17 Nov. 1562–16 Nov. 1563
6	17 Nov. 1563–16 Nov. 1564
7	17 Nov. 1564–16 Nov. 1565
8	17 Nov. 1565–16 Nov. 1566
9	17 Nov. 1566–16 Nov. 1567
10	17 Nov. 1567–16 Nov. 1568
11	17 Nov. 1568–16 Nov. 1569
12	17 Nov. 1569–16 Nov. 1570
13	17 Nov. 1570–16 Nov. 1571
14	17 Nov. 1571–16 Nov. 1572
15	17 Nov. 1572–16 Nov. 1573
16	17 Nov. 1573–16 Nov. 1574
17	17 Nov. 1574–16 Nov. 1575
18	17 Nov. 1575–16 Nov. 1576
19	17 Nov. 1576–16 Nov. 1577
20	17 Nov. 1577–16 Nov. 1578
21	17 Nov. 1578–16 Nov. 1579
22	17 Nov. 1579–16 Nov. 1580
23	17 Nov. 1580–16 Nov. 1581
24	17 Nov. 1581–16 Nov. 1582
25	17 Nov. 1582–16 Nov. 1583
26	17 Nov. 1583–16 Nov. 1584
27	17 Nov. 1584–16 Nov. 1585
28	17 Nov. 1585–16 Nov. 1586
29	17 Nov. 1586–16 Nov. 1587
30	17 Nov. 1587–16 Nov. 1588
31	17 Nov. 1588–16 Nov. 1589
32	17 Nov. 1589–16 Nov. 1590
33	17 Nov. 1590–16 Nov. 1591
34	17 Nov. 1591–16 Nov. 1592
35	17 Nov. 1592–16 Nov. 1593
36	17 Nov. 1593–16 Nov. 1594
37	17 Nov. 1594–16 Nov. 1595
38	17 Nov. 1595–16 Nov. 1596
39	17 Nov. 1596–16 Nov. 1597

ELIZABETH I–cont.

40	17 Nov. 1597–16 Nov. 1598
41	17 Nov. 1598–16 Nov. 1599
42	17 Nov. 1599–16 Nov. 1600
43	17 Nov. 1600–16 Nov. 1601
44	17 Nov. 1601–16 Nov. 1602
45	17 Nov. 1602–24 March 1603

JAMES I

1	24 March 1603–23 March 1604
2	24 March 1604–23 March 1605
3	24 March 1605–23 March 1606
4	24 March 1606–23 March 1607
5	24 March 1607–23 March 1608
6	24 March 1608–23 March 1609
7	24 March 1609–23 March 1610
8	24 March 1610–23 March 1611
9	24 March 1611–23 March 1612
10	24 March 1612–23 March 1613
11	24 March 1613–23 March 1614
12	24 March 1614–23 March 1615
13	24 March 1615–23 March 1616
14	24 March 1616–23 March 1617
15	24 March 1617–23 March 1618
16	24 March 1618–23 March 1619
17	24 March 1619–23 March 1620
18	24 March 1620–23 March 1621
19	24 March 1621–23 March 1622
20	24 March 1622–23 March 1623
21	24 March 1623–23 March 1624
22	24 March 1624–23 March 1625
23	24 March 1625–27 March 1625

CHARLES I

1	27 March 1625–26 March 1626
2	27 March 1626–26 March 1627
3	27 March 1627–26 March 1628
4	27 March 1628–26 March 1629
5	27 March 1629–26 March 1630
6	27 March 1630–26 March 1631
7	27 March 1631–26 March 1632
8	27 March 1632–26 March 1633
9	27 March 1633–26 March 1634
10	27 March 1634–26 March 1635
11	27 March 1635–26 March 1636
12	27 March 1636–26 March 1637
13	27 March 1637–26 March 1638
14	27 March 1638–26 March 1639
15	27 March 1639–26 March 1640
16	27 March 1640–26 March 1641
17	27 March 1641–26 March 1642
18	27 March 1642–26 March 1643
19	27 March 1643–26 March 1644
20	27 March 1644–26 March 1645
21	27 March 1645–26 March 1646
22	27 March 1646–26 March 1647
23	27 March 1647–26 March 1648
24	27 March 1648–30 Jan. 1649

THE COMMONWEALTH

Kingship was abolished in 1649 after the execution of Charles I on January 30th. Thereafter, in the Commonwealth period, calendar years only were used.

When Charles II was restored to the throne in 1660, his regnal years were dated from 1649, as if he had succeeded immediately on his father's death.

CHARLES II

12	29 May 1660–29 Jan. 1661
13	30 Jan. 1661–29 Jan. 1662
14	30 Jan. 1662–29 Jan. 1663
15	30 Jan. 1663–29 Jan. 1664
16	30 Jan. 1664–29 Jan. 1665
17	30 Jan. 1665–29 Jan. 1666
18	30 Jan. 1666–29 Jan. 1667
19	30 Jan. 1667–29 Jan. 1668
20	30 Jan. 1668–29 Jan. 1669
21	30 Jan. 1669–29 Jan. 1670
22	30 Jan. 1670–29 Jan. 1671
23	30 Jan. 1671–29 Jan. 1672
24	30 Jan. 1672–29 Jan. 1673
25	30 Jan. 1673–29 Jan. 1674
26	30 Jan. 1674–29 Jan. 1675
27	30 Jan. 1675–29 Jan. 1676
28	30 Jan. 1676–29 Jan. 1677
29	30 Jan. 1677–29 Jan. 1678
30	30 Jan. 1678–29 Jan. 1679
31	30 Jan. 1679–29 Jan. 1680
32	30 Jan. 1680–29 Jan. 1681
33	30 Jan. 1681–29 Jan. 1682
34	30 Jan. 1682–29 Jan. 1683
35	30 Jan. 1683–29 Jan. 1684
36	30 Jan. 1684–29 Jan. 1685
37	30 Jan. 1685–6 Feb. 1685

JAMES II

1	6 Feb. 1685–5 Feb. 1686
2	6 Feb. 1686–5 Feb. 1687
3	6 Feb. 1687–5 Feb. 1688
4	6 Feb. 1688–11 Dec. 1688

INTERREGNUM

12 Dec. 1688–12 Feb. 1689

WILLIAM and MARY

1	13 Feb. 1689–12 Feb. 1690
2	13 Feb. 1690–12 Feb. 1691
3	13 Feb. 1691–12 Feb. 1692
4	13 Feb. 1692–12 Feb. 1693
5	13 Feb. 1693–12 Feb. 1694
6	13 Feb. 1694–27 Dec. 1694

WILLIAM III

6	28 Dec. 1694–12 Feb. 1695
7	13 Feb. 1695–12 Feb. 1696
8	13 Feb. 1696–12 Feb. 1697
9	13 Feb. 1697–12 Feb. 1698
10	13 Feb. 1698–12 Feb. 1699
11	13 Feb. 1699–12 Feb. 1700
12	13 Feb. 1700–12 Feb. 1701
13	13 Feb. 1701–12 Feb. 1702
14	13 Feb. 1702–8 March 1702

ANNE

1	8 March 1702–7 March 1703
2	8 March 1703–7 March 1704
3	8 March 1704–7 March 1705
4	8 March 1705–7 March 1706
5	8 March 1706–7 March 1707
6	8 March 1707–7 March 1708
7	8 March 1708–7 March 1709
8	8 March 1709–7 March 1710
9	8 March 1710–7 March 1711
10	8 March 1711–7 March 1712
11	8 March 1712–7 March 1713
12	8 March 1713–7 March 1714
13	8 March 1714–1 Aug. 1714

GEORGE I

1	1 Aug. 1714–31 July 1715
2	1 Aug. 1715–31 July 1716
3	1 Aug. 1716–31 July 1717
4	1 Aug. 1717–31 July 1718
5	1 Aug. 1718–31 July 1719
6	1 Aug. 1719–31 July 1720
7	1 Aug. 1720–31 July 1721

GEORGE I-cont.

8	1 Aug. 1721–31 July 1722
9	1 Aug. 1722–31 July 1723
10	1 Aug. 1723–31 July 1724
11	1 Aug. 1724–31 July 1725
12	1 Aug. 1725–31 July 1726
13	1 Aug. 1726–11 June 1727

GEORGE II

1	11 June 1727–10 June 1728
2	11 June 1728–10 June 1729
3	11 June 1729–10 June 1730
4	11 June 1730–10 June 1731
5	11 June 1731–10 June 1732
6	11 June 1732–10 June 1733
7	11 June 1733–10 June 1734
8	11 June 1734–10 June 1735
9	11 June 1735–10 June 1736
10	11 June 1736–10 June 1737
11	11 June 1737–10 June 1738
12	11 June 1738–10 June 1739
13	11 June 1739–10 June 1740
14	11 June 1740–10 June 1741
15	11 June 1741–10 June 1742
16	11 June 1742–10 June 1743
17	11 June 1743–10 June 1744
18	11 June 1744–10 June 1745
19	11 June 1745–10 June 1746
20	11 June 1746–10 June 1747
21	11 June 1747–10 June 1748
22	11 June 1748–10 June 1749
23	11 June 1749–10 June 1750
24	11 June 1750–10 June 1751
25	11 June 1751–10 June 1752
26	11 June 1752–21 June 1753
27	22 June 1753–21 June 1754
28	22 June 1754–21 June 1755
29	22 June 1755–21 June 1756
30	22 June 1756–21 June 1757
31	22 June 1757–21 June 1758
32	22 June 1758–21 June 1759
33	22 June 1759–21 June 1760
34	22 June 1760–25 Oct. 1760

GEORGE III

1	25 Oct. 1760–24 Oct. 1761
2	25 Oct. 1761–24 Oct. 1762
3	25 Oct. 1762–24 Oct. 1763
4	25 Oct. 1763–24 Oct. 1764
5	25 Oct. 1764–24 Oct. 1765
6	25 Oct. 1765–24 Oct. 1766
7	25 Oct. 1766–24 Oct. 1767
8	25 Oct. 1767–24 Oct. 1768
9	25 Oct. 1768–24 Oct. 1769
10	25 Oct. 1769–24 Oct. 1770
11	25 Oct. 1770–24 Oct. 1771

GEORGE III-cont.

12	25 Oct. 1771–24 Oct. 1772
13	25 Oct. 1772–24 Oct. 1773
14	25 Oct. 1773–24 Oct. 1774
15	25 Oct. 1774–24 Oct. 1775
16	25 Oct. 1775–24 Oct. 1776
17	25 Oct. 1776–24 Oct. 1777
18	25 Oct. 1777–24 Oct. 1778
19	25 Oct. 1778–24 Oct. 1779
20	25 Oct. 1779–24 Oct. 1780
21	25 Oct. 1779–24 Oct. 1781
22	25 Oct. 1781–24 Oct. 1782
23	25 Oct. 1782–24 Oct. 1783
24	25 Oct. 1783–24 Oct. 1784
25	25 Oct. 1784–24 Oct. 1785
26	25 Oct. 1785–24 Oct. 1786
27	25 Oct. 1786–24 Oct. 1787
28	25 Oct. 1787–24 Oct. 1788
29	25 Oct. 1788–24 Oct. 1789
30	25 Oct. 1789–24 Oct. 1790
31	25 Oct. 1790–24 Oct. 1791
32	25 Oct. 1791–24 Oct. 1792
33	25 Oct. 1792–24 Oct. 1793
34	25 Oct. 1793–24 Oct. 1794
35	25 Oct. 1794–24 Oct. 1795
36	25 Oct. 1795–24 Oct. 1796
37	25 Oct. 1796–24 Oct. 1797
38	25 Oct. 1797–24 Oct. 1798
39	25 Oct. 1798–24 Oct. 1799
40	25 Oct. 1799–24 Oct. 1800
41	25 Oct. 1798–24 Oct. 1801
42	25 Oct. 1801–24 Oct. 1802
43	25 Oct. 1802–24 Oct. 1803
44	25 Oct. 1803–24 Oct. 1804
45	25 Oct. 1804–24 Oct. 1805
46	25 Oct. 1805–24 Oct. 1806
47	25 Oct. 1806–24 Oct. 1807
48	25 Oct. 1807–24 Oct. 1808
49	25 Oct. 1808–24 Oct. 1809
50	25 Oct. 1809–24 Oct. 1810
51	25 Oct. 1810–24 Oct. 1811
52	25 Oct. 1811–24 Oct. 1812
53	25 Oct. 1812–24 Oct. 1813
54	25 Oct. 1813–24 Oct. 1814
55	25 Oct. 1814–24 Oct. 1815
56	25 Oct. 1815–24 Oct. 1816
57	25 Oct. 1816–24 Oct. 1817
58	25 Oct. 1817–24 Oct. 1818
59	25 Oct. 1818–24 Oct. 1819
60	25 Oct. 1819–29 Jan. 1820

GEORGE IV

1	29 Jan. 1820–28 Jan. 1821
2	29 Jan. 1821–28 Jan. 1822
3	29 Jan. 1822–28 Jan. 1823
4	29 Jan. 1823–28 Jan. 1824
5	29 Jan. 1824–28 Jan. 1825
6	29 Jan. 1825–28 Jan. 1826
7	29 Jan. 1826–28 Jan. 1827
8	29 Jan. 1827–28 Jan. 1828
9	29 Jan. 1828–28 Jan. 1829
10	29 Jan. 1829–28 Jan. 1830
11	29 Jan. 1830–26 June 1830

WILLIAM IV

1	26 June 1830–25 June 1831
2	26 June 1831–25 June 1832
3	26 June 1832–25 June 1833
4	26 June 1833–25 June 1834
5	26 June 1834–25 June 1835
6	26 June 1835–25 June 1836
7	26 June 1836–20 June 1837

Reproduced from C R Cheney's *Handbook of Dates* (1978 edition) by kind permission of the Royal Historical Society.